Epidemiology in health care planning

A guide to the uses of a scientific method

Edited for the International Epidemiological Association
and the World Health Organization by

E.G. KNOX

Assisted by

R.M. ACHESON

D.O. ANDERSON

T.W. BICE

K.L. WHITE

Oxford
OXFORD UNIVERSITY PRESS
New York Toronto
1979

Oxford University Press, Walton Street, Oxford OX2 6DP

OXFORD LONDON GLASGOW NEW YORK
TORONTO MELBOURNE WELLINGTON CAPE TOWN
IBADAN NAIROBI DAR ES SALAAM LUSAKA ADDIS ABABA
KUALA LUMPUR SINGAPORE JAKARTA HONG KONG TOKYO
DELHI BOMBAY CALCUTTA MADRAS KARACHI

ISBN 0 19 261221 2

Typeset by Hope Services, Clifton Hampden
Printed in Great Britain
by J.W. Arrowsmith Ltd., Bristol

Oxford Medical Publications

Handbooks sponsored by the IEA and WHO

Other volumes in this series:

Foreword

Dr. B. SKRINJAR-NERIMA
Chief, Development of Health Statistics
World Health Organization

Dr. H. P. CAIN II, World Health Organization

This handbook is an important contribution to a growing literature that strives to construct a rational basis for setting priorities and allocating scarce health care resources. It discusses ways in which the scientific method and logic can be introduced into the practical arena of planning health services. Planning has been described as 'negotiating the future' and depends in both developed and developing countries on the judicious use of quantitative methods based on sensibly employed health statistics. These in turn are derived from population surveys and service record sources. In the acquisition, aggregation, and analysis of these data, principles and methods of epidemiology are employed. It is these principles and methods which this volume attempts to interpret for health planners. At the same time, the authors seek to make the perspectives and problems of planning more comprehensible to epidemiologists. This book should prove useful to practitioners, teachers, and students in the fields of epidemiology and health statistics, and to other professional groups concerned with the planning and administration of health services.

Although guided by an editor and an editorial board, this volume is the product of a multidisciplinary group comprising 27 contributors from 15 countries who worked for two years through correspondence, several small meetings, and two large working conferences. It is the result of effective cross-national collaboration between the International Epidemiological Association, the World Health Organization, and the United States Department of Health, Education, and Welfare and represents a broad range of perspectives, interests, and skills.

Acknowledgements

This report is made pursuant to Contract #HRA 230-76-0079. The amount charged to the Department of Health, Education, and Welfare for the work resulting in this report (inclusive of the amounts so charged for any prior reports submitted under this contract) is $71 750. The names of the persons, employed or retained by the contractor, with managerial or professional responsibility for such work, or for the content of the report, are Kerr L. White, M.D. and E. George Knox, M.D. Dr. Thomas McCarthy and Mrs. Helen Thornberry were the project officers.

Additional support was provided by The Commonwealth Fund, The Esther A. and Joseph Klingenstein Fund, Inc., the Institute for Health Care Studies of the United Hospital Fund, and the Milbank Memorial Fund, all of New York City.

Secretarial and editorial assistance were provided by Sheila Allen and Eileen Armstrong.

Contents

List of contributors

Professor E. G. Knox (editor-in-chief), Department of Social Medicine, University of Birmingham, Edgbaston, Birmingham, B15 2TJ, England

Professor R. M. Acheson (editor), Department of Community Medicine, University of Cambridge, New Addenbrooke's Hospital, Hills Road, Cambridge, CB2 2QQ, England.

Dr. D. O. Anderson (editor), Clinical Professor, Department of Health Care and Epidemiology, University of British Columbia, Vancouver, British Columbia, Canada V6T 1W5.

Professor T. Bice (editor), Deputy Director, Institute for Health Care Studies, United Hospital Fund of New York, 3 East 54th Street, New York, N. Y. 10022, U.S.A.

Professor K. L. White (editor), Director, Institute for Health Care Studies, United Hospital Fund of New York, 3 East 54th Street, New York, N. Y. 10022, U.S.A.

Dr. A. I. Adams, Director, Division of Health Services Research, Health Commission of New South Wales, 9–13 Young Street, Sydney, N.S.W. 2001, Australia.

Professor C. Buck, Department of Epidemiology and Preventive Medicine, Faculty of Medicine, University of Western Ontario, London, Ontario, N6A 5B7, Canada.

Professor M. A. Faghih, Professor of Epidemiology, School of Public Health, University of Teheran, Teheran, Iran.

Dr. T. Fülöp, Director, Division of Health Manpower Development, World Health Organization, 1211 Geneva 27, Switzerland.

Dr. J. J. Guilbert, Chief Medical Officer for Educational Planning, Division of Health Manpower Development, World Health Organization, 1211 Geneva 27, Switzerland.

Dr. A. S. Häro, Chief, Department of Planning and Evaluation, National Board of Health, Helsinki 53, Finland.

Dr. B. S. Hetzel, Chief, C.S.I.R.O., Division of Human Nutrition, Kintore Avenue, Adelaide 5000, Australia.

Dr. M. L. Kakande, Associate Professor, Institute of Public Health, Faculty of Medicine, Makerere University, P. O. Box 7072, Kampala, Uganda.

Dr. B. M. Kleczkowski, Chief Medical Officer, Resource Group, Div. of Strengthening of Health Services, World Health Organization, 1211 Geneva 27, Switzerland.

Professor J. K. Kostrzewski, Department of Epidemiology, State Institute of Hygiene, 24 Chocimska Street, 00-791 Warsaw, Poland.

Dr. P. E. Leaverton, Associate Director for Research, National Center for Health Statistics, 3700 East-West Highway, Hyattsville, Maryland 20782, U.S.A.

Professor S. K. Lwanga, Department of Preventive Medicine, Faculty of Medicine, Makerere University, P. O. Box 7072, Kampala, Uganda.

Professor L. M. F. Massé, Professor of Statistics, Public Health & Epidemiology, Ecole Nationale de la Sante Publique, 35.043 Rennes-Cedex, France.

Dr. A. Mejia Vanegas, Chief Medical Officer, Health Manpower Systems, Division of Health Manpower Development, World Health Organization, 1211 Geneva 27, Switzerland.

Ms. J. H. Murnaghan, Assistant Professor of Health Services Administration, School of Hygiene and Public Health, The Johns Hopkins University, 615 North Wolfe Street, Baltimore, Maryland 21205, U.S.A.

Ms. J. Roberts, London School of Hygiene & Tropical Medicine, Centre for Extension Training in Community Medicine, 31 Bedford Square, London, WC1B 3EL, England.

Professor R. Sharma, Professor & Head and Principal, Department of Social and Preventative Medicine, S. N. Medical College, Jodhpur 342003, India.

Dr. B. Skrinjar-Nerima, Chief, Development of Health Statistical Services, World Health Organization, 1211 Geneva 27, Switzerland.

Dr. A. Sonis, Director, Regional Library of Medicine and Health Sciences, Pan American Health Organization, Caixa Postal 20.381 — Vila Clementino, 04023 São Paulo, S.P. Brazil.

Mrs. H. Thornberry, Assistant to the Director, Department of Health, Education, and Welfare, Bureau of Health Planning and Resources Development, 3700 East-West Highway-Center Building, Hyattsville, Maryland 20782, U.S.A.

Professor W. E. Waters, Professor of Community Medicine, South Block, Southampton General Hospital, Southampton SO9 4XY, England.

Dr. D. Williams, Director, Health Services Management Centre, University of Birmingham, Egbaston, Birmingham, B15 2TJ, England.

Introduction: Scope and objectives

The purpose of this book is to describe the contribution of the scientific discipline of epidemiology to the operational discipline of health care planning.

Neither discipline is new, nor is the idea of applying one to the other, but the systematic development of the relationship is recent. Many epidemiologists and health statisticians have up to now seen their roles in quite limited terms, employing a rather narrow repertoire of investigative and analytical techniques and addressing a circumscribed range of questions. Few of them accepted the challenges of health care planning and some of them questioned the legitimacy of participating in the solution of current health care problems. Some still do. Administrators engaged in planning health services for the most part accepted the circumscriptions of epidemiology in the terms which its practitioners themselves set. When the administrators were chiefly engaged in managing the financial and institutional frameworks from which health care services operate, rather than with the standards and effectiveness of the care itself, they showed little concern about the extensions of interest of a few epidemiologists into health care. In recent years, however, movement on both sides has resulted in a growing overlap of perceived roles, a growing need for partnership, and an attendant danger that rivalries and misunderstandings might cloud a potentially fruitful relationship.

So far as epidemiology is concerned the movement may be seen as the latest stage of a long-continued development. The discipline escaped from the restrictions of the epidemic and infectious diseases many years ago. Its methods were successfully applied to the investigation of chronic diseases, to physical disabilities and impairments, and to a variety of developmental, behavioural, occupational, and adaptive problems. The results of many such investigations found outlets in a range of disease control measures—although results and recommendations arising from others still await effective implementation—but the emphasis remained, as previously, on prevention. In the course of these developments, some epidemiologists turned their attention to the effects of medical procedures upon the incidence and severity of certain disease processes. As well as developing and testing effective vaccination and chemotherapeutic regimes their studies led to the elucidation of iatrogenic diseases (i.e. diseases caused by medical care) and the re-evaluation of many traditional but ineffective medical and surgical activities. Others paid special attention to the reliability of medical observations and developed the methods and approaches of measuring and controlling errors. These new traditions of work effected major changes in the way medicine is practised, in the way it is conceptualized and presented to its users, and in the way that doctors are educated.

In one sense, however, epidemiology remained within its traditional boundaries. The determinants of health, sickness, and social performance, and the prevention of disease, remained its chief concerns and the growing involvement in health care focused upon diagnostic and therapeutic procedures rather than upon total services. This containment was partly due to the restricted range of technical methods which most epidemiologists used, partly to the physical separation of epidemiologists from decision-making processes, and partly to a restrictive concept of the proper place of a scientific discipline in relation to administration. The reasons for the subsequent changes are complex but stem in part from technical developments in the handling of information, and requirements for large-scale information systems. The growing use of the 'systems' concept in epidemiology and in administration eroded their traditional segregation and blurred distinctions between professional roles. At the same time the increasing use of computer methods in the analysis of epidemiological material assisted in the systematization of the methods employed; epidemiology was no longer definable in terms of its detailed subject matters (e.g. infectious diseases) but in terms of its methods, its models, and the fact that it was concerned with populations. Thus, an epidemiologist must now be defined simply as someone who practises the techniques of epidemiology, whether his background be in statistics, in economics, in operational research, in sociology, in information technology, in clinical science, in clinical practice, or in empirical field studies. For many epidemiologists with traditional backgrounds, the attitudes which previously favoured scientific detachment from the imperatives of a decision making environment or the maintenance at most of a passive advisory role, have been replaced by a desire for involvement in the processes of designing services to meet the medical needs they had already measured and analysed.

These movements have been neither uniform nor universally accepted and have varied in detail, direction, and purpose in different geographical and political contexts, and they have interacted with the varying concepts and expectations of scientific and administrative participants. Difficulties arose when epidemiologists were asked to assist decisions which available data would not easily bear; or to accept work timetables set by a planning problem, but not easily reconcilable with the requirements of scientific accuracy and rigour. Administrative bodies were sometimes unwilling to expose the subtleties of policies or of policy formulation to objective study, mathematical analysis, or computer simulation; in some situations the idea of exposing services to data-based evaluations was almost heretical. The relationship between epidemiology and administration is still a turbulent one, and more so in health care planning than in health planning as a whole.

The separation of health care planning from health planning as a whole, is arbitrary. Although this separation is the basis of the present book we recognize that its desirability is debatable. Its utility can be argued on the grounds that measures for maintaining health, and measures for providing health care, are in many countries administered through different pathways. It is also possible to argue conversely. Many health problems require a conscious choice between solutions provided through health care services and those provided through other routes. This is especially relevant where resources are limited, but is becoming increasingly pertinent in the more affluent countries where the health care approach appears to be encountering diminishing returns.

Our main reason for focusing upon health-care planning is because the role of epidemiology here is to some extent still contentious. In the fields of health maintenance and prevention, epidemiological methods have enjoyed a long-standing recognition, but with respect to health care planning there are still some rough edges. In some quarters, it must be said, the distinction between the two is not accurately recognized and the importance of health care as a determinant of health has been widely misunderstood and exaggerated. One of our secondary purposes must be to assist in this delineation.

A valid declaration of the uses of epidemiology in health care planning must be applicable in different places, in different political contexts, and in different areas of medical practice. It must take account of the varied pace and direction of movement in many environments. It must provide a conceptual synthesis and at the same time identify any conflicts of ideas or of professional expectations which need to be reconciled. The objectives of the book will be met only if its contributors succeed in providing insights both into the philosophy of their science and into the practicalities of its application. Since the subject matter relates to an interface between two main professional activities, administrative and epidemiological, it must be constructed with the needs of at least two groups of readers in mind.

The book has not be constructed as a technical guide. Although the epidemiologist's skills and methods and the types of information which he uses are described, this is mainly for the purpose of exposing the scope and credentials of the discipline in relation to planning. Nor is the book designed as an exposition of the arts of planning; descriptions of the planning process are provided only to display the context in which the epidemiologist will have to operate. We wish to demonstrate to planners and administrators what a good edpidemiologist can supply, to show those who construct administrative and planning mechanisms where the epidemiologist must be fitted in, to show educators the educational needs of those who contribute to the planning process, and to show those who collect and supply data for planning purposes, how the results of their labours are employed. In each case we wish to promote progressive development and change, and we shall not complain if our readers notice an element of advocacy.

The pursuit of these aims has influenced the style and the structure of the book and has presented its contributors and editors with many problems. They are problems without solutions, and we shall be unable to instruct or to please all of our readers all of the time. It is impossible to provide a demonstration of the validity and utility of a professional approach without probing in some depth, but difficult to do this without a technical penetration which is outside our main objectives. We have therefore made wide use of illustrative examples. They are included in order to give point to more general and more abstract ideas and to demonstrate in a wide range of circumstances what complementations of technique are necessary for epidemiologists who wish to enter the health care field.

The objectives of the book are reflected in its structure. Part I is devoted to an analysis and discussion of the planning processes within which a variety of workers, including epidemiologists, have to work. Part II discusses information, the common raw material both of the administrator/planner and the planner/epidemiologist. Part III displays the scientific and technical basis of epidemiology and describes the kinds of problem with which it can cope. Part IV describes the working relationships between epidemiologists, and others engaged in planning, together with the ways in which they must be trained and educated and the manner in which the subject must be advanced, if the discipline is to be effectively used.

The order in which the book should be read is to some extent optional and the choice will be guided by careful perusal of the list of contents. Readers who do not know what epidemiology *is* and who want a definition, may wish to turn first to Part III, while those who have had little exposure to the conceptual background or the terminology of planning should begin at the beginning, with Part I. Those who expect to find the 'information' sandwich of Part II indigestible might first read Parts I and III (or III and I). There are options also *within* the parts, and textual guidance is provided in the introductory paragraphs. It may be a good plan, for most readers, to read the introductory pages of each section before embarking on the book as a whole. Those with more regard for outcome than for process might like to concentrate immediately upon Part IV, where most of our recommendations will be found.

The four parts contain some repetition and we hope our readers will not find this too irksome. The repetition arose initially because the drafts were developed in parallel rather than serially, and each group of authors saw their section as an independently valid statement which relied neither upon the text which preceded it nor that which followed. The desirability of providing for alternative orders of reading led us to preserve the free-standing characteristics of the four main themes and, consequently, a certain amount of repeated material.

PART I

Health care planning

1. Social choice

The focal point of planning is the act of choosing between alternative means towards desired ends. In indviduals this is seen simply as rational behaviour. Social planning, by analogy, may be seen as rational behaviour among groups and communities. It is the process through which collective goals are pursued and appropriate methods agreed. Health planning, and within it health care planning, are subsets of this process.

Social planning is not, however, a simple question of adding together a set of individual rationalities. The formulation of goals and objectives requires the reconciliation of opposing views, and the planner has to deal with irrationality as well as with consistent but conflicting proposals. This is inherently a political process, and social planning requires mechanisms and structures through which information, authority, and preferences may be aggregated, and through which agreed strategies may subsequently be disaggregated to create plans of implementation. The planning process, the administrative structures, the administrative mechanisms, and the interactions between them may be conceived, together, as a planning system. A discussion of this system and of its component parts provides the subject matter for this part.

Part 1 is arranged to cover each of these points in turn. In Chapter 2 we describe social planning systems in ideal and general terms, covering the principal features common to all situations. In Chapter 3 we analyse the planning process itself, identifying and describing its component parts. In doing so we draw progressively upon illustrations from the health care field. In Chapter 4 we describe models of administrative mechanisms and structures which show how the exercise of rational choice may be facilitated or impeded by its social and political contexts. In doing so we hope to develop further the general notion of a 'system' which, as we have already said, is central to the theme. In Chapter 5 we shall define the domain of health care planning, locating it in the larger context of health planning, and identifying two principal outlets, namely institutional and functional planning. Finally, in Chapter 6 drawing upon these descriptions and analyses, we identify the types of skills, knowledge, and information required by those contributing to health care planning.

2. Planning systems

A system may be defined as a set of interrelated elements, each contributing to the accomplishment of an aggregate activity. In social planning systems the elements and the relationships consist of the resources, the technologies, the activities, and the actors. Social planning requires transactions not only between elements *within* the planning system, but between elements on each side of its boundaries. For this reason it is properly described as an 'open' system. In describing an open system it is necessary to define both kinds of relationships, namely between elements within the system, and between elements of the system and elements of the environment. The notional separation of an open system from its environment is arbitrary and hinges upon the purposes for which the system is conceived. So too is the separation of sub-systems from the larger system which forms *their* environment.

The purposes of a planning system, as well as its organization, resources, and technologies, are shaped by the environment within which it functions. The objective realities faced by a society and its prevailing social and political values jointly determine the nature and scope of the problems to which planning is addressed, which actors participate in the planning process, the degree to which planning is integrated across sectors, and the powers which the planners may rightfully exercise. In modern socialist nations, for instance, the primacy accorded to collective welfare and ownership legitimizes governmental planning and control over all sectors of the economy. The planning function is vested in government and the powers of the state are employed to implement comprehensive plans. By contrast, in nations where private ownership and enterprise are highly valued, planning is typically fragmentary rather than comprehensive, with only weak governmental enforcement.

The variety of circumstances and of social and political structures in different societies precludes a general definition of the terms in which the boundary between a planning system and its environment may be recognized. Pragmatically we must usually identify a planning system with the specifiable administrative mechanism and structure which it serves. The effectiveness of the planning system, including any supportive research and evaluative activities, depends upon the accurate delineation of this mechanism, and of its power pathways. The administrative structure provides the links to the environment through which flow the values, information, standards, resources, and the authority to implement the plans. It encompasses formal and informal relationships among planners, between planners and the public and the government, and between the planners and the objects of control. The degree to which an idealized planning process is effectively realized in practice depends upon the success with which these relationships are defined and developed.

3. The planning process

3.1. THE CIRCULAR PRINCIPLE

The planning process consists of a series of steps, which are followed in a more or less systematic way. The series begins with the identification of problems, and passes through a consideration of alternative strategies for ameliorating the problems, to the choice of a preferred means. The chosen programme is then implemented, and finally evaluated. Evaluation raises fresh questions, so the process is inherently cyclical; it is represented in Fig. 1.

In practice the environment may constrain the process in several ways and at several points and it may not proceed in the orderly and idealized cycle depicted in Fig. 1. Steps may be omitted, some may be attempted twice, and there may be obstructions and delays and simultaneous activities in different parts of the cycle. Each stage in the cycle may resolve itself into a sub-cycle. In this chapter, however, we shall disregard these distortions in order to develop our description of the components and we shall return later to a discussion of the ways in which the continuity and the effectiveness of the process may be constrained.

3.2. SITUATION ANALYSIS

The occasion and the stimulus for planning is the recognition that a current situation is undesirable, or may become so, or that an alternative would be better. This recognition may arise within the planning system itself, or in its 'environment', entering through the lobbying of interest groups, through external administrative direction, through public outcries, or through legal decisions. Whatever its source, it demands an analysis of the situation.

Such analysis requires, first, a definition of the problem, and an assessment or measurement of its extent, severity, causes, and impacts upon the community. The problem may have been posed and formulated in relatively exact terms. Typically, however, it will be stated in value-laden terms with imprecise magnitudes which must be translated into programmatic and quantitative terms. For example, dissatisfactions with an abortion service may be expressed in terms of 'a woman's right to choose' without reference to the facts of the law as it stands, the existing rules of procedure and whether they can be changed, or to the distribution and adequacy of existing facilities.

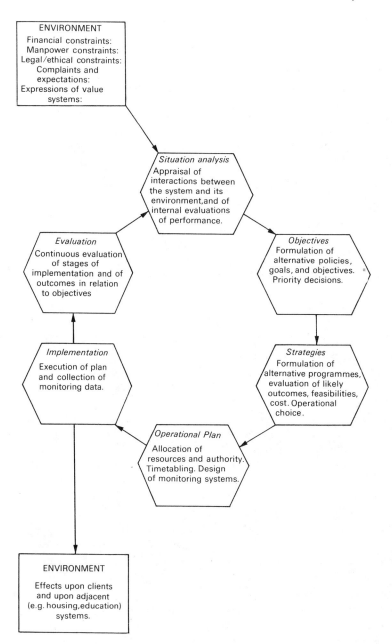

Fig. 1. Cybernetic planning cycle

It may be a perfectly valid complaint but translation of problems presented in this way into a format capable of promoting action will usually require reference to some standard of optimality, normality, or desirability which can be understood within a frame of reference broader than that of the immediate problem.

3.3. PRIORITIES

Competing demands for limited resources restrict the responsiveness of the planning system. Indeed, competition for time and study forces planners to select for immediate attention only a few of the problems brought to their notice and to avoid or defer action on the others. The problems themselves (let alone the possibilities of their solution) must therefore be assigned a position in a ranking of priorities. These processes occur at all planning levels and follow typically upon a complex interplay of political, professional, administrative, and consumer pressures in which interest groups lobby for favoured programmes. At governmental levels, for example, the needs of the community for health care services will be considered in relation to competing needs for defence, law enforcement, education, housing, employment, consumer goods, social security, and so on. Priorities are forged, here, from a blend of compromises, rules of thumb, and tradition. Ultimately they are expressed objectively in the budgetary allocations of resources to competing needs (Wildavsky 1975).

Decisions to channel resources into one sector or another are rarely made in an explicit fashion in which the benefits of relative marginal investments (e.g. between education and health) are openly considered. Health planners are seldom directly involved in determining what resources are allocated to health or in determining the relative dispositions between health and health care; the latter distinction may not even be appreciated at the levels where the decisions are made.

Within any given sector the principles and criteria on which priority decisions are made may differ at different levels of administration. Planning bodies controlling centrally supported services (e.g. education, health care, police) will be concerned with public accountability. They will be under pressure, for example, to ensure a reasonable degree of geographical equity of resource distribution. At peripheral levels, by contrast, the main concern will be to adapt the service to individual or to small-group needs. Intermediate levels will be driven by a search for efficiency and by a desire to accommodate the conflicting demands and constraints of upper and lower levels. The criteria of equity, of efficiency, and of responsiveness to individual need—all of them legitimate—may nevertheless conflict and themselves require priority decisions. The priority ordering may differ at different levels, and the tendency for large organizations to split into layers may be a reflection of this fact.

At every level, however, priority decisions will always be based upon a blend of factual evidence about the past and present, upon attempts to predict the future, upon tradition and law, upon changing value systems and expectations, and upon the degree to which resources are thought to be transferable from one use to another. The accommodation of incommensurables is necessarily inexact and the outcome springs from a bargaining process rather than an objective formula; that is, whatever the administrative structure and mechanism within which priority setting takes place, it is always inherently political in nature. Because priorities are established repeatedly at different levels of government and different levels of administration, and among different agencies with competing interests, each giving different weights to the elements on which a decision may be made, statements on priorities are often inconsistent, and sometimes incompatible. They are likely to change, moreover, between the point where a plan is developed and the time at which it comes to fruition. The planning process must seek, so far as possible, to be cohesive and comprehensive and to allow for change; but the planner must at the same time recognize that there are always limits to the consistency with which priorities can be stated, and in the degree to which they can be met.

3.4. GOALS AND OBJECTIVES

Because priorities are usually established in rather general terms it is necessary, before action can be taken, to translate them into specific goals and objectives. They must be designed to indicate clearly which activities are to be initiated and what end states are to be achieved.

Terms such as goals, objectives, targets, and aims are often used interchangeably, and there are no exact agreed definitions. Where more than one is used in a single context a hierarchy of specificities may be implied. Thus, a general goal is translated into a set of more precise objectives, and these in turn into even more specific targets or aims. Within these various usages, however, it is generally agreed that when properly formulated they must possess one essential attribute. That is, they must be stated in terms of an activity which is itself 'visible', or whose effects are visible. Such a formulation is usually described as a 'behavioural' objective. If a goal is not set in such terms, then it must be restated in terms of sub-objectives which are so stated. A behavioural objective may stress the activities of providers (e.g. improved services to the elderly), of recipients of services (e.g. increased uptake of preventive services), or the effects of provision and usage upon social or biological behaviour (e.g. reduced mental illness). Goals that are not expressed in terms of verbs whose actions can be observed, and preferably measured, preclude subsequent evaluation of the programme designed to meet them. At operational levels a well-specified objective indicates (1) the 'dimension' in which changes are to occur, (2) its measure or indicator, (3) the time period in which the change is to occur, (4) its direction, and (5) magnitude (DHEW, 1976). A commitment 'to reduce infant mortality by 1980 from 19 to 15 deaths per 1000 live births', relies upon all of these elements, and provides the necessary criteria for evaluating progress towards its attainment.

Goals may be expressed in a range of dimensions; in health care planning they may be stated in terms of attack rates of disease, indicators of health status, measures of accessibility, standards of health care services, financial inputs, staffing ratios, consumer satisfaction, and equity, among others. These various criteria are sometimes classified as goals of 'input', goals of 'process', and goals of 'output'.

In complex social systems the economic concepts of input and output may be difficult to apply and, if naively used, can be misleading. In health and health care planning we prefer, ideally, to state our objectives in such terms as the reduced incidence or prevalence of sickness, or in terms of case fatality rates, durations of disability, successful social adaptation, and the like. However, when a planning activity is limited only to part of the system, as it often is, the aims may have to be set in 'process' terms. Thus the output of one activity may form the input to the next. An improved volume and quality of health education may be regarded, from one point of view, as a desirable outcome. From another, it represents an investment and a cost against which the benefits of improved health will have to be balanced. Both points of view are legitimate in their proper contexts.

Furthermore, there are aspects of health care whose objectives are difficult to express in terms of objective outputs. The common element of all consultative medicine is the provision of advice (whatever else may or may not be provided) and many sick people require shelter, social contact, and other forms of support, irrespective of efficacy. Their provision may be regarded legitimately as an end in itself, at least in the short term. These problems are more likely to trouble health care planners than those responsible for health planning as a whole. For the larger activity there can seldom be much doubt about the manner in which the goals must be set.

3.5. CHOICE OF STRATEGIES

The choice of a strategy or programme from a range of alternatives may be made simply in the light of its feasibility. If only one plan is feasible because of cost or staffing constraints then, apart from details, the question is simply whether or when to move. If more than one alternative is feasible then the choice must be made in terms of such standards as their probable effectiveness, acceptability, timings, economy, adaptability to available staffing or premises, or administrative ease and efficiency. However, there may be serious difficulties in applying indices of these kinds and in calculating objective ratios between the various kinds of benefit (medical benefit, cash saving) and the various kinds of disbenefit (financial cost, length of interval between expenditure and outcome, medical hazards). It may become necessary, then, to undertake a service on a limited scale before deciding whether and how to implement it in a definitive form. Even here there are problems—many health care services have been structured upon the common but false assumption that all necessary research will be carried out before decisions about implementation are faced. Research staffs and research mechanisms are commonly separate from service administration, and it may be difficult to develop a limited service within the normal administrative context and yet keep it under firm research/developmental control. Yet research is normally a prerequisite of any output-related evaluation. These difficulties, and the need to overcome them, provide a major stimulus for this book.

It is useful at this point to draw a qualitative distinction between the different terms in which the 'outputs' of services and their components may be expressed. There are three concepts in current use denoted by the terms effectiveness, efficacy, and efficiency. They are not used with complete consistency but in most usages the term 'efficiency' is related to internal (i.e. process) targets while the other two terms, 'efficacy' and 'effectiveness' are based upon external (i.e. output) targets. That is, efficiency is a measure of the ratio between the quantity and quality of services provided, and the cost of providing them. 'Effectiveness' and 'efficacy' relate outcomes, expressed in terms of improved health status, to inputs, expressed in terms of the service provided. Although the distinction between effectiveness and efficacy is not universally agreed or observed, one school of thought limits the term 'efficacy' to the assessment of particular medical and surgical procedures considered in isolation; the term 'effectiveness' is reserved for describing the performance of total services applied to defined target populations.

Unfortunately, conceptual difficulties remain and exact treatments of health care planning problems remain difficult. The concepts of cost efficiency, cost effectiveness, and cost benefit, borrowed from other contexts, are frequently used in ways which are mutually inconsistent and which do not necessarily correspond with the concepts outlined above. The non-commensurate nature of the inputs and outputs of health care systems create serious difficulties. Real-life situations, requiring marginal decisions with marginal effects, frequently encounter complex non-linear relationships between additional inputs, additional benefits, and additional costs. Formal maximization of any particular index or ratio can lead to absurdities. For example, in cervical cancer screening, the first Pananicolaou smear will give a higher yield than the second one, and the second one a higher yield than the third, and so on. A programme consisting of a single smear per woman would maximize the cost–benefit ratio; but a recommendation based upon this maximization would be absurd.

We can perhaps best summarize these problems in the conclusion that the field of strategic analysis in health care planning is presently undeveloped and requires a period of major participatory activity and experiment on the part of several professional groups before it can be improved.

3.6. EVALUATION

Evaluation is the process of relating the outcome of planned activities to their objectives. Although evaluation is often treated as an after-the-fact attempt to determine whether a programme 'worked', this is only one of the meanings of the term. Planning and evaluation must be managed as a continuous interactive process leading to continual modification both of objectives and plans. It is sometimes then referred to as 'monitoring'. This kind of evaluation is valuable to managers as well as to planners and enables them to be sure that resources are not being misdirected, and that mid-course modifications of programmes provide appropriate gains. In addition to showing whether a programme has worked, detailed evaluation provides the basis for checking and refining its theoretical basis. Without factual checks and refinements of the theory behind the programme, it may be impossible to proceed rationally to the setting of new goals and objectives, and choosing among new alternatives. For example, the initial theoretical basis for a whooping cough vaccination programme is provided by serological studies and controlled studies of efficacy, in a context with a high risk of exposure. A period of experience of a large-scale service may refine this knowledge, providing more precise estimates of levels of protection and the risks of side-effects. During a subsequent period of declining risk of exposure,the balance between benefit and hazard will change and it may appear desirable to alter doses, or ages of immunization, or the strain of organism used for the vaccine, or some combination. Meanwhile, the ecosystem is changing, with a changing age distribution of exposure, a changing distribution of family size, and, possibly, a change in the organism itself. Unless the service is continually monitored a situation may arise in which concern about the ill effects of the vaccine results in pressures to discontinue the service and demands decisions which existing know-ledge is unable to guide. Crises of this kind have in fact occurred.

Opportunities for effective evaluation depend first upon how explicitly the objectives were defined in advance. Only too often the evaluator finds that the aims were implied rather than written down and finds himself forced into making *post hoc* formulations. He is likely to be influenced in these judgements by what has in fact occurred. Successful evaluation may also depend upon whether the means of evaluation were built into the design of the programme before it was implemented and upon the degree of control exercised over the programme itself and its data collection systems. Another important consideration is the degree to which the evaluator can himself manipulate the service and perhaps build into it the possibility of comparing alternative regimes.

'Evaluation' may also be used in the sense of evaluating proposals, rather than programmes which have already been started, that is, *'evaluation in advance'*. The planner *forecasts* potential outcomes of alternative policies, based upon previous experience and upon a theoretical model of the system, and evaluates each of them. When projecting needs for particular types of hospital services, for instance, the planner may be able to identify population parameters which 'predict' changing uses of out-patient services, under observed circumstances where supplies of in-patient services vary. This theoreti-cal model may then be applied to populations with new characteristics, and the model used to predict the outcomes of different mixes of in-patient and out-patient services. Models of these kinds are widely used by operational research workers (−'operations research' in the USA).

The special contribution of the epidemiologist in such applications will relate to the development and assessment of services defined in functional rather than in purely institutional terms. He will be con-cerned with services provided for different types of client and different types of sickness problems and he will be concerned with the standards and the outcomes of care as much as with their provision.

The disciplines of operational research, behavioural science, and economics deal more directly with issues of procedural and economic efficiency, but, in matters pertaining to the impact of alternative programmes upon health, the epidemiological approach is essential.

In situations well endowed with expert staff, the approach might be provided by a professional epidemiologist or medical statistician. In many situations, however, the requirement implies a need for some epidemiological training for general administrators, for clinicians, or for others in charge of planning.

3.7. NORMALITY, NORMS, GUIDELINES, AND STANDARDS

We have up to now used the term 'standards' in a rather general sense. The term has been used to cover criteria of desirability, efficiency, effectiveness, appropriateness, acceptability, equity, and so on. We hope in this section to develop the concept of a 'standard' and of several related terms, in a more exact manner. In doing so we shall encounter semantic problems; in the health care field one frequently encounters terms transported from clinical science which, in their new context, may be misunderstood. They include 'normal', 'norm', 'guideline', and 'standard'. In addition there is sometimes confusion between 'standards' and 'standardization'.

'Normal', in the field of health, has long held the special meaning of being free of any particular disease or disability. Later, the concept was attached to quantitative as opposed to purely qualitative criteria, such as temperature, blood pressure, or concentrations of body-fluid constituents. Normality became associated with 'average' and with statistically calculated ranges of deviation from that average. This led to conceptual difficulties.

Thus, the mean value for serum cholesterol in a general population sample from Framingham, Massachusetts (Dawber *et al.* 1957) was 225 mg per cent and examination of risks of ischaemic heart disease at different cholesterol levels led the investigators to classify values above 260 mg per cent as 'abnormal' and the remainder as 'normal'. Later it was shown that there is a continuous gradient of risk of ischaemic heart disease over most of the scale, and this led to a re-examination of the widely used concept of a 'normal range'. Nevertheless limits of 'two standard deviations around the mean' were still being used, for clinical purposes, in the late 1960s (Murphy and Abbey 1967). The word 'normal' was still being confused with the word 'usual'.

This semantic fallacy has been transferred on many occasions into the field of planning health services. In 1948 the National Health Service (NHS) in Britain, took over existing hospitals. They had been built and managed by a wide variety of local agencies without any semblance of a national plan, and bed provisions varied widely in different regions. The response of the appropriate government department to the new requirement for a national policy was perhaps predictable; it treated the national average as the 'norm'. If we accept the connotation of the word 'norm' as 'a standard which may have guiding or regulating functions', and if it is in fact used for these purposes, we can easily recognize the inertial properties of the circular pressures which results. They ignore needs; they limit change.

Neither the clinical nor the planning dilemma can be solved without reference to external criteria, for example the incidence of ischaemic heart disease or the assessed needs for hospital beds. Reference to external criteria is also a prerequisite of any bench mark from which the effectiveness or quality of a service can be assessed. The definition of reference criteria of these kinds is the essence of the concept of a 'standard'. Standards, in this sense, do not depend upon what is 'normal' or 'usual' and they do not, in fact, necessarily depend upon observations. Sometimes they must be established and used before their effectiveness or practicability in controlling or evaluating a service can be measured.

Traditionally, standards have been established by authority, with the backing of the law. Standard weights and measures are an example. Implicitly, such standards are usually *minimum* standards and it is important in planning contexts to realize that other kinds of standards exist. Three main usages can be distinguished.

They are (i) 'minimum' or 'minimum acceptable' standards, (ii) 'ideal' standards, and (iii) 'reference' standards. The meaning of minimum standards is self-evident although they may of course be expressed in terms of maximum values, for example a case-fatality rate for children with intussusception, the national perinatal mortality rate, the incidence of skin sepsis in a neonatal care unit, or the upper limits of waiting times for out-patient appointments. In each of these cases the 'ideal' standard might be regarded as zero. In planning contexts the term 'ideal standard' is sometimes used perjoratively, implying a requirement for something more concrete, more specific, and dated (see § 3.4). The choice between minima, ideals, and operational targets, introduces the notion of a *scale* of standards. A scale carries no moral, legal, normative, or target connotations and the definition of reference standards is purely a technical problem, a question of accurate definition and of utility. For example, security standards for confidential medical records may consist of a set of procedural guidelines providing successive levels of protection. A general practice record system would probably adopt one level; a psychiatric clinic, a venereal diseases clinic, or a contraceptive service for unmarried women would probably adopt another. There is much that can be done to improve the quality of health care services through the careful definition and adoption of procedural standards such as these.

Standards of performance (output) are more difficult to formulate than standards of procedure (process). They are difficult to conceptualize, and costly (and touchy) to measure. They are likely to require operational trials and evaluation. An example would be the problem of identifying health outcomes suitable for evaluating the co-ordinating effect of a new polyclinic, where the professional personnel previously worked in an uncoordinated manner. The investigator would probably rely first upon a combination of indices, including measures of accessibility, waiting times, customer satisfaction, and descriptions and enumerations of the kinds of activity in which doctors, nurses, and other personnel previously, and subsequently, engaged. He would not know which were useful criteria for comparing these performances until he had completed at least a pilot investigation, and the establishment of these criteria would constitute the main results of this part of his study. He would not, however, in any strict sense have measured the performance of the polyclinic in terms of true outputs. Whether because of technical or conceptual difficulties, performance estimates are frequently described in terms of the standards with which care is delivered, rather than the results of the care. Such standards are not to be despised and in sensitive situations they may be the only ones which can be satisfactorily defined with some hope of acceptance.

4. Administrative contexts, structures, and processes

4.1. PLANNING CONTEXTS

The frame of reference within which the planning process takes place is determined by the wider social context. A contrast between two levels of societal organization will serve to illustrate this point. In a relatively primitive society health planning may concentrate chiefly upon improving water supplies and sanitation. This is suited both to the relative poverty of the society and to its unstructured nature. That is, there are social as well as financial limits to the possibilities of providing individual social and health care. Sanitation programmes require individuals neither to modify their social or cultural patterns, nor to undertake specialized roles, nor to forgo personal incomes or possessions. Where individuals resist adopting recommended sanitary practices, legal powers may be required to enforce compliance but this may represent the limits of practical corporate responsibility. The planning of personal health care services, by contrast, depends upon the existence of specialized personnel and upon the responses of the providers of the services as well as the recipients and upon the allocation or re-allocation of resources. This kind of planning depends upon the possibility of mobilizing political support and presupposes a (relatively) highly-structured administrative system for social services in general.

Hyman (1976) has identified four basic kinds of planning contexts which he designates as (1) systems, (2) partnerships, (3) alliances, and (4) individual actions. Systems planning agencies conform most nearly to what we typically call 'management', in that authority over all resources is concentrated at the apex of a control structure. Implementation of plans is achieved in such structures by executive command and budget allocations. This type of planning is approximated in some Eastern European nations where health services are provided by the state, and within government-owned facilities such as Veterans Administration hospitals in the United States.

In planning systems based on partnerships, authority is divided among different agencies or levels of government. Objectives and means are established collectively through bargaining and negotiation and, once established, are implemented by central authorities through budget allocations and executive commands. The health care planning processes of Sweden and the United Kingdom illustrate this form of partnership planning.

Health care planning based on alliances depends upon voluntary agreements among actors (individual or group), each of which retains its authority to act independently. Goals are arrived at through 'consensus-oriented' compromises, and plans are implemented voluntarily. In some instances, legal constraints are imposed on the actors' freedom to engage in certain behaviours, and these are typically imposed by government agencies. Such is the prevailing pattern in the United States, where regional Health Systems Agencies containing representatives of all interested parties are charged with developing area-wide plans and advising state agencies on regulatory matters.

Finally, in planning by individual action, the planning agency is merely a resource used by individual organizations to help them achieve their own aims. Lacking authority over its clients, and having only limited advisory roles with higher authorities, planning in this context is usually aimed at short-term resource acquisition. The Regional Medical Programs and Experimental Health Services Delivery Systems in the United States employed this form of planning during the late 1960s.

These styles of health care planning confront the planner with different opportunities and constraints. Systems planning offers close contact with policy makers who both select the goals and control the means necessary to implement plans. Under these circumstances planners will be called upon to conduct large-scale policy analysis and to engage in technical details of resource allocation. Where planning is accomplished through partnerships among identified actors and constituencies, planners' roles will be more varied, for each participant will contribute his own plans to a bargaining process which ultimately produces plans that are binding upon him. Those who represent the participants are expected to devise plans that best serve their particular interests and to negotiate with central authorities compromises to be reflected in the final plan. Partnership planning therefore requires political as well as technical skills.

Where planning is carried out through alliances, a major problem is the absence of consensus about goals and a lack of institutional mechanisms for developing them. Since alliances have few direct powers over participants, the planners' political skills in mobilizing public sentiment are likely to be as valuable as their technical skills. In such settings, attention to long-range, system-wide planning is frequently compromised by the necessity to attend to short-term incremental adjustments involving recalcitrant and independently powerful institutions.

4.2. ORGANIZATION

The above models indicate the technical and political skills needed by planners in different circumstances, but the success of a planning effort cannot rest on these skills alone. It depends also on how resources, expertise, and tasks are organized. A central notion of organizational analysis has been that of 'structure', with differentiation of tiers of authority, divisions of labours, and defined relationships, rules, and procedures. These are the chief ingredients of classical management theory and they are valid as far as they go. A characteristic weakness, in the past, has been to suppose that management structures are essentially free from the influences of an external environment. Communications (inputs, outputs) across the system boundary were well defined, but the idea that the internal organization itself should be capable of adapting to changes in styles of communication was not well catered for. In practice, of course, the structure itself must change in response to social and technological changes, to changes in the degree and pattern of profressional and technical diversity, and to increasing complexity in the pattern of integration between the system and its environment.

These pressures tend to go together. In stable situations with little professional and technical diversity and little need for integration, planning will involve rather routine techniques which can be applied through conventional, hierarchical management structures. In more complex situations, where a rapid development of social service agencies interacts with the traditional responsibility of health care services for the care of the elderly, or the physically disabled, a complicated system of liaison arrangements may become necessary. Professional staff in health care systems tend to be centrifugally distributed and to exhibit high degrees of job differentiation. This, together with rapid technical change, imposes a requirement for integration at peripheral rather than at central levels. Hierarchical modes of management must usually be reinforced by other arrangements. The planning and administrative structuring itself must therefor respond.

Modern management theory promises no universally valid principles for handling these issues, but there are suggestions that planning agencies are more effective when organized as matrix systems than as traditional, hierarchical structures. The distinction is illustrated in Fig. 2. Organization A is based on a division of services on institutional lines, and organization B in more functional terms, but both are hierarchical and neither would be easily responsive to the administrative and planning needs expressed in the other. By contrast, a matrix

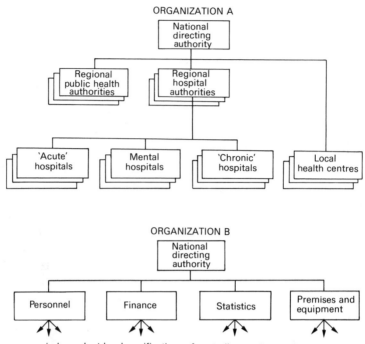

.... independent local ramifications of centrally coordinated functions

Fig. 2. Alternative hierarchical representation of the same system.

organization form (Fig. 3—organization C), perhaps with more than two dimensions, explicitly defines the planning and managerial roles as intersections and provides a basis for integration. As Lawrence and Lorsch (1967) illustrate, the communications and decision making problems of complex systems can be further eased by the introduction of other integrating devices. They postulate the need for 'enabling' roles, wholly or partly free of hierarchical accountability, perhaps established in permanent cross-unit planning and management teams.

4.3. RATIONALITY AND NON-RATIONALITY IN DECISION MAKING

In earlier sections of Part 1 we have referred to 'the planner' as if he were a single individual acting for and by himself. Discussions of process have tended to follow the assumption of individual rationality. There are, however, dangers in these assumptions. As we stated at the outset, social planning is not a simple question of adding or averaging individual rationalities.

When an individual engages in rational planning he constructs a unique priority ordering, first of alternative goals and then of alternative means. They reflect his system of values and his personnel and

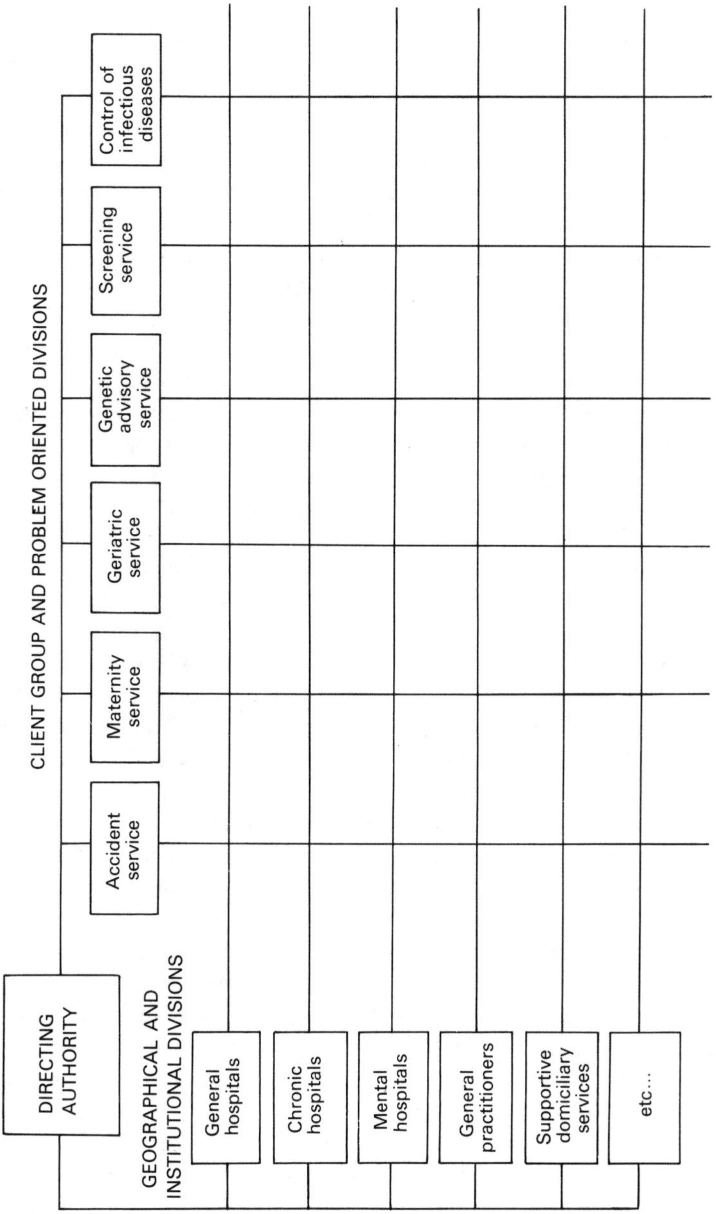

Fig.3. Matrix representation of administrative structure (Organization C).

material resources. Group planning is, however, more complex, unanimity is rare, and it is unlikely that the final outcome will replicate directly the choice of any individual of the group. That is, the result will not depend upon the rationality of any of the individuals from whose views it was constructed. Whenever there is some centralization of authority, as in all forms of social planning, inward (afferent) flows require the aggregation of information and of individual values, and outward (efferent) flows require the disaggregation of policy, of general objectives, and of authority. Thus, a planning body will be responsible for gathering and reconciling preferences and priorities of competing individuals and groups, creating from these a collective decision, and issuing commands derived from it. There is danger of irrationality in all these situations.

The process of arriving at a collective decision is basically extralogical. In the absence of imposed value judgements there can be no uniquely 'correct' ordering of societal preferences. The actual outcome, known in welfare economics as a Pareto-Optimal Solution, suffers from a demonstrable limit upon its rationality; that is, it is fully rational only when those who benefit by it do so with no losses to those not benefited. When benefits and costs of decisions fall unevenly on groups, additional ethical principles are required in order to guide decisions. Rawls (1973) for instance, argues that collective decisions are fair only when the situation of the least advantaged members of society is made at least no worse by them. Others arguing from the ethical premise of the supremacy of individual rights contend that fairness requires freedom from collective decisions that coercively effect transfers among individuals and groups (Nozick 1974).

Although the inherent dilemmas arising from these problems of aggregating individual and group preferences are common to all social planning, they are more troublesome in health care planning than in environmental or public health planning. In the latter, decisions regarding the allocation of resources produce outcomes that are valued in the aggregate more than by individuals themselves, and societies establish programmes that individuals would not otherwise pursue. By contrast, health care planning more often involves transfers of prerogatives from identifiable groups to others, whether they be from one class of providers to another, from providers to consumers, or from one group of consumers to others.

Tools of rational decision making such as cost-benefit analysis are only partially rational when applied to transfer decisions. They apply directly to the selection, from among alternatives, of the means to achieve an objective on behalf of an identifiable group. The decisions whether it is more efficient to treat end-stage renal disease by transplant or dialysis, and whether it is preferable to use resources for these patients, or for others, supply examples. The question whether it is 'better' to provide more maternal and infant care services or more extended geriatric care services, forces choices among alternatives that variously benefit the young or the elderly. Appearances of rationality derived from a demonstration that the maternal and infant care programmes will avert a greater loss of life-years, carry the implied assumption that additional years of life are equivalent at all ages. This, of course, is a value judgement and as such is not verifiable, and it must follow that any process leading to the favouring of the one programme over the other, is inherently non-rational.

Non-rationality will appear as a recurrent theme throughout this book. It provides an important ingredient of the problem of managing the working interface between scientists and non-scientists in the field of health care planning.

5. Applications to health and to health care services

Although our account has drawn upon illustrations from the health field, it has been laid out in general terms which might be applicable to any social planning purpose. At this point we turn towards health planning, and within it health care planning, in a more specific sense.

We drew a distinction between health planning and health care planning in the Introduction and in § 3.3, and this distinction is essential to an understanding of this book. They differ not only in their range of purposes but in their instrumental pathways. Health planning operates through modifying any or all of the determinants of health, including the physical and social environments and patterns of individual and group behaviour, as well as through the personal health services. By contrast, health care planning focuses on the latter, attempting to select volumes and configurations of facilities, personnel, technologies, equipment, and services which will best meet the needs of defined populations within limits imposed by resources and acceptability.

Relative emphases upon the two processes stem from the nature of the threats to the health of the population. Generally speaking, investment in health care will give the highest marginal returns in communities and nations which have solved the fundamental problems of subsistence and of environmental control, but have not advanced to the point where health is threatened by what Fuchs (1972) has labelled 'diseases of living'. Investment in the fundamental needs of housing, education, agricultural production, and sanitation will produce greater improvements in the health of populations ravaged by ignorance, starvation, and environmentally borne agents than will investment in health care. Interestingly, there may be a tertiary stage of the balance equation, appropriate to nations which have passed through both the elementary sanitary/subsistence stage, and the stage of investing in health care. Investment in health care may become progressively less efficient, with diminishing marginal returns, and may then justify or enforce an awakened interest in preventive measures aimed at changing life-styles, promoting knowledge about self-care, and eliminating more complex or subtle environmental hazards to health.

Unfortunately, the distinction and the relationship between health and health care procedures have not always been well understood and this had led to inappropriate balances between them; also, within health care, between preventive and therapeutic services, and between primary (general/community) and secondary (specialist/hospital) activities. In Ethiopia, for example, and contrary to the advice of the World Health Organization a decision was taken to establish a major medical school at Addis Ababa. This concentrated in a single metropolitan community the resources previously spread over the entire nation of thirty million people.

Elsewhere there are signs of a sharpened understanding of these problems as expressed in a number of significant reports and publications (e.g. Lalonde 1974; McKeown 1976; DHSS 1976), and as a range of administrative actions further testify (e.g. health manpower legislation in the United States). There is a growing realization, in the circumstance which these authors analysed, that recent investments in health care have not provided the health improvements that many people had expected. Furthermore current levels of health care expenditure in many countries, running at 7–9 per cent of the Gross National Product, are encountering competitive pressures which are likely to bar their further advance.

We were conscious, in constructing this book, that our chosen terms of reference effectively evaded these issues and crises of direction: issues requiring accurate identifications of the role of therapeutic medicine in each of its varying social settings. The isolation of health care planning, for separate consideration, was clearly artificial. We must plead, simply, that our thesis is concerned with the narrower question, and that this stems from current positions and developments in the contributions of epidemiology.

5.2. INSTITUTIONAL AND FUNCTIONAL HEALTH CARE PLANNING

Health care systems differ greatly in different countries, but have one fact in common: they are always extremely complex. The complexities themselves display a consistent feature: that is, every health care system can be conceived or described in terms of several alternative structures. From one point of view the service is a set of buildings and staff with defined and related functions; from another, it is a set of professional groups (e.g. doctors and nurses) and of unionized labour (drivers and porters); another structural concept relates to a series of general and special clinical functions related by referral pathways; from another point of view still, the system may be defined in terms of its sources of finance, with voluntary, municipal, private, and national components.

The purpose of a planning operation takes on a different meaning within each of the structures and the terms on which an epidemiologist may be involved depend crucially upon the adopted image. We referred to these issues briefly in § 4.2 in the concept of a 'matrix organization'. Figure 3 illustrates the idea in terms of an extremely simple and stylized two-dimensional arrangement in which individual roles are defined as matrix intersections. Health care systems are always of this type, except that they are usually multi-dimensional. This is an intrinsic fact, whether or not it is recognized in formal representations of the administrative and planning mechanism. Indeed, it is a characteristic of health care systems that the realities are always much more intricate than formalized representations suggest.

It is useful, for purposes of understanding the planning role of the epidemiologist, to divide these coexisting alternative structures and activities into two main classes. They are reflected in the title to this section, namely 'institutional' and 'functional' planning. Institutional planning relates to the terms and manner in which staff are employed, the processes whereby buildings are acquired and maintained, and the manner in which the hierarchical layers of an administration maintain their mutual relationships and fulfil their mutual commitments. It is concerned with hospitals, with general practices, with health centres, with training schemes, with transport, with finance, and with managerial and legal accountability. If there is a single criterion by which its activities are judged, that criterion is efficiency. Functional planning, by contrast, operates within a structure defined in problem-orientated terms. It is concerned in its more general forms with services for client groups such as the aged, children, or the disabled, and in more specific terms (for instance) with the management of traffic casualties, acute abdominal emergencies, pneumonia, measles, and whooping cough, with hernias and haemorrhoids, defects of eyesight and hearing, and the effects of industrial hazards. If these activities have a single criterion, then it is effectiveness.

Neither system can work on its own. The two complex taxonomies interact and constitute a matrix which at any one time may be beyond ready comprehension and which in any case is constantly changing. A wide variety of scientific, planning, and managerial tasks are located at the various intersections; at times several people will be involved in a single task; other tasks will go unmanned or even unnoticed.

The relationship between the institutional and the functional frameworks will differ in different situations. Where health care provision operates in a relatively unstructured environment, the functionally-defined services may be seen as primary, although possibly fragmentary. For example, there may be a range of privately-operated primary care and specialist services; mechanisms of administration and finance will be seen as secondary, and central responsibility for planning and for evaluation will be weak.

In complex administrations, by contrast, particularly those where both resources and public accountability pass through governmental channels, the institutional framework may be seen as 'primary'. One of the functions of the institutional mechanism, here, is to develop and provide the framework within which functional planning and development can take place. It also provides the aggregative mechanism through which locally determined needs are assembled, so that influence can be brought to bear upon the amount of the total resource allocated to health care.

Whatever the order of primacy awarded to the institutional and functional concepts it is important to remember that it is within the second of these that the purposes, the outputs, and the true justification of the total system are to be found. If the institutional services of the health care system fail to define, develop, and evaluate services which may be understood in functional terms, then they fail in their ultimate purpose. Unfortunately, especially where the institutions are designed with political aims in mind—the achievement of equity of access irrespective of ability to pay, for example—this can happen only too easily. Administrative structures may then be seen by the various professional groups as an embodiment of inertia and as a source of resistance to development and change. If this is to be avoided and the requirements of smooth day-to-day running reconciled with the requirements of continued development and adaptation, then a well judged and fruitful balance between the two activities must be achieved. It is a difficult task. It is also of prime importance in the context of this book because planning which takes place within the functional framework is seen as the special province of epidemiology and of some of the related scientific disciplines. Indeed, the balance between institutional and functional planning represents very clearly the interface, to which we earlier referred, between the interests and activities of managers and epidemiologists. This is a theme to which we shall return.

6. Knowledge, skills, and style

Planning has been defined as 'negotiating the future'. It is based upon administrative power, whether this be formally designated through political or legal processes, or obtained adventitiously through technical control of money or information. At both levels the effective use of planning power demands a facility with numbers and a capacity for the complex art and quasi-science of estimating, projecting, and predicting. A good intuitive appreciation of quantitative relationships is required (over and above a facility for arithmetic) and the planner must frequently be prepared to be 'roughly right rather than precisely or elaborately wrong'. A good sense of risk-taking and a probabilistic view of alternative choices are further desirable attributes. As in other fields, good judgement comes from experience, and experience comes from bad judgement, and developing the art of planning must be regarded as an iterative process. Constant corrections are required by new circumstances, be they political, technological, or scientific, and an accurate sense of current developments and a high level of current knowledge in each of these fields, must be maintained.

The skills and knowledge required of individual contributors to the planning process will depend upon the prevailing and traditional style in which the planning operation is carried out in the particular location. Where the style is 'impressionistic' or 'idealistic', few scientific skills will be called for, or even tolerated. Planning, here, is based upon more or less arbitrary decisions stemming from experience, tradition, and broad guesses about future needs and possibilities, using minimal amounts of formal information. Objectives will tend to be vague or 'Utopian', standards will be set in general rather than in operational terms, and 'implementation' may rely excessively upon exhortation. Practical planning will have to be carried out covertly, with little material support, and will call upon personal skills of persuasion and a degree of subtlety. Planning systems with strong central direction will call upon a different range of skills and knowledge, from those where the main drives are peripheral. There will be differences also between those situations where the 'matrix' structure of the service is recognized and reflected in its administrative arrangements and those situations where one or other of the alternative hierarchies attains particular dominance. Nevertheless, there is a range of scientific skills and knowledge which are always necessary in some degree if the planning process is to respond to real needs. Some of these requirements are epidemiological and statistical in nature. They include a basic knowledge of the structure of the recipient population including its age/sex distribution, its social characteristics and its social geography. It is necessary to know the frequencies of the different main forms of sickness and disability and, again, their geographical and social distributions. It is necessary to assemble a statistical characterization of the resources of the service in terms of buildings, staff, finance, etc., and in terms of the volumes and types of activities which it currently undertakes. In all three areas of knowledge, demography, morbidity, and resources, current information must be supplemented by projections of likely movements in the future. Finally, it is necessary to assemble numerical estimates describing more complex concepts such as the volumes and types of medical and social 'needs', of 'demand', of 'economic costings', of 'priorities', of 'constraints upon growth', of 'outcomes', and so on. Rational planning demands all of these elements. It cannot take place if they do not exist.

The acquisition, processing, indexing, storing, retrieval, interpretation, and presentation of this knowledge requires special techniques and skills. They include data-acquisition and data-processing techniques and a range of statistical analytical methods such as standardization, correlation and dependency analysis, geographical and temporal display methods, error measurement and control, sampling techniques, and so on. The interpretation of data in terms which find practical application is a skilful, intuitive process requiring a broad, and often detailed knowledge of the biological background, and of practical operational issues, as well as of statistical method, and these particular areas require the services of skilled scientists. The biological issues, in particular, are central to the epidemiologist's craft.

Finally, planning involves prediction, and all prediction is difficult. Major step-wise changes are the least predictable of all including catastrophies, major technological and scientific breakthroughs, and major turnabouts in social attitudes (e.g. to abortion, or to the privacy of medical records). That such events will occur is reasonably certain, but their precise nature, location, and timing are extremely difficult to forecast. Wide general knowledge and good intuition may be the only guides. Incremental changes, however, are more tangible and their prediction is an obligatory rather than an optional planning activity. The skills involved include those of operational research and computer-programming and the construction and usage of more or less complex mathematical and computer-simulation models. The

particular skills required of epidemiologists centre upon the introduction of realistic representations of biological variables into these
modelling processes.

The development of improved styles of planning, and the proper
use of the scientific contribution, hinge very largely upon the open-
ness with which all these activities are carried out. In closed and
relatively autocratic systems, there is little stimulus to explain how a
given conclusion was reached, or who reached it, or what alternatives
were considered. However, systems which are more open, and where
priorities and conclusions may be questioned, demand more formal
and more readily communicable expressions of the bases of decision
making. The exact format will depend very largely upon the pattern
of accountability which has become established. Where the pattern
of accountability is representative and political the main terms of
expression will relate to social criteria such as accessibility, equity,
and the protection of the individual against injustice or incompetence.
Where the accountability is directed through professional/scientific
pathways, the appropriate forms of expression will relate to criteria
such as effectiveness, efficiency, the maintenance of high standards,
and the reconciliation of needs and resources. There have been
steady improvements, in many parts of the world, in the ways in
which social and technical accountability are managed. This has
occurred despite the increased complexity and expense of the
administrative and planning processes and it is a trend which is
likely to continue. Movements in the area of professional and scientific
accountability are of special interest in relation to the themes discussed
in this book. It is this movement which has driven epidemiologists,
other scientists, and administrators into a common area of concern.
It explains also the format of the book. In Part II we discuss the
knowledge necessary for planning; in Part III we describe the epidemiological skills necessary for bringing this knowledge to bear upon
health care problems and the forms which its applications take; in
Part IV we describe the working and training relationships which are
necessary to bring it all about.

PART II

Health care information

7. Information and information systems

7.1. DEFINITIONS

The term 'information' covers a range of meanings. It is used first in a colloquial sense to denote knowledge, and carries the notions of pertinence to a problem and of interpretation; it may be distinguished thus from mere 'data' (Murnaghan 1974). It is used next in a more technical manner to denote the vehicle which carries the knowledge; in this sense we imagine a 'material' which may be communicated, transmitted, received, recorded, written, and read, also converted (transduced) between one physical representation and another. It may be visual, auditory, tactile, etc; it may be literate, numerate, or graphical.

In all its senses, however, information is understood as a representation of reality. It 'stands for' something apart from itself, and it exists entirely within a universe of symbols.

It represents not only the static facts of the external world but also its operations and its activities, and the utility of information both in science and in social planning depends upon the postulate that operations (e.g. arithmetic) carried out upon elements of information will correspond consistently with real actions carried out upon real objects.

The information used in health care planning represents the states, events, identities, procedures, relationships, and processes, which constitute the system whose maintenance and modification are intended. First it records a range of biological phenomena, the events of falling ill, of getting better, of adapting to chronic sickness or disability, and responding to treatment. Information referring to groups may be derived from these primary data, and 'secondary' information of this kind describes the natural history of disease, the efficacy of therapy, the effectiveness of health care services, and the hazards of medical and surgical procedures. Secondly, the information base of health planning records a range of administrative and operational procedures and of group data derived from them; they relate to financing and budgeting operations, the control of waiting lists, the training of medical orderlies, the dynamics of demand and supply in blood transfusion services, the migration of doctors, the salaries of nurses, the design of premises, the quality control of biochemical services, and so on. In its entirety, therefore, the information base represents all the systems within which the planner works including both the operational and planning systems of the service, and the biological and social systems with which they interact.

Information can also be seen as a system in its own right, and the design, management, control, and usage of information systems is a central interest of administrators and scientists. They are concerned both with the knowledge stored within the system, sometimes referred to as an 'intelligence system', and with the processes of acquiring, coding, aggregating, reducing, and redistributing information—processes often referred to collectively as an 'information engineering system'. Those parts of the engineering system involving the electronic or mechanical handling of data are referred to as an 'automatic data processing (ADP) system'.

Within this complex range of usages and activities there is considerable scope for confusion, both of terminology and of concept. In this book we use the term 'information system' rather generally, to include both 'engineering and processing' (where the emphasis is upon methods and patterns of handling), and 'intelligence' (where the emphasis is upon the content and the meaning).

In the remainder of Chapter 7 we shall develop the 'systems' concept of information further, looking both at its structure and its processes. In Chapters 8 and 9 (to which some readers may prefer to jump) we examine 'intelligence systems', with descriptions both of uses and sources. Later, in Chapter 10, we reconsider information systems in an integral manner, and examine the ways in which they are managed.

7.2. THE STRUCTURE OF HEALTH CARE INFORMATION

Health care information is a highly structured material. This is true at least of the literate and numerate forms of information with which planners are concerned. The notions of sequence, of hierarchical structure (bracketing, nesting), of linkage (e.g. cross-indexing), and of the existence of different information-types, are essential to understanding as well as to effective recording and retrieval. Thus, basic elements are grouped into reports, reports into records, records into files, and the files into a total record system. The terms 'file' and 'record' are used without consistent meaning, except that the former is generally understood in more global terms than the latter. Within this understanding however, one user's file is another user's record and a total system may contain as many layers and levels (sub-systems, sub-files, sub-records, etc.) as are necessary to its purposes.

The most precisely definable parts of an information structure are the basic 'elements' of which the lowest-level 'records' are composed. Basic elements are always defined, either explicitly or implicitly, as doublets. The doublets comprise a 'quality' and a 'value'. An example of a linked set of such doublets, that is a record, might be /History of present complaint : shot in the eye by an arrow // date: 14 October 1066 // condition on admission : dead // name : Harold/.

There are strong precedents for this doublet construction in the field of natural science where, classically, an 'element' is defined as a quality with a quantity. An example would be /mass of the earth in grams: $6 \cdot 0 \times 10^{27}$/. This classical/quality: quantity/formulation limits itself to measured numerical values (i.e. 'real numbers') whereas the broader/quality: value/formulation can accommodate values of other types. They include identifiers (e.g. names or admission numbers), taxonomic class labels (e.g. diagnoses), and texts (history of present complaint). The importance of these distinctions appears when we come to consider the various kinds of manipulations which can be carried out upon them; certain kinds of technical operations may be carried out only upon certain types of values. For example, arithmetic operations can be carried out upon 'real numbers' and 'integers' but not upon numerical identifiers. Also the consequences of errors are quite different for each value-type, as are the methods of controlling them. Analysis in these terms became important with the development of computer techniques and each of the value-types is recognized, and catered for, within the main computer languages.

In many instances, of course, only the 'value' is actually written down and its meaning or 'quality' is understood through reference to rules of interpretation contained within a computer programme, or in the minds of those responsible for making written records. Doublet-format descriptive elements may also refer to aggregated data-sets (e.g. records, files) as well as to observations made upon individuals. Statistical estimates (e.g./mean weight at birth in kg:$3 \cdot 3$/) are of this type. In this sense, we may assemble records of file-descriptors, and even files of such records. Statistical digests and intelligence systems may be viewed in this light.

7.3. PROCESS

The materials of chief interest to health care planners are 'digested' information-sets referring to groups rather than to individuals. For information sources outside the health care system itself, responsibilities for processing and analysis will rest with scientists and other staff over which the health care planner has no direct control.

For information sources *within* the health care system, however, there is a definable responsibility for all the processes associated with data acquisition and data analysis. There is also a direct responsibility, here, for efferent as well as for afferent information processes including both the distribution of intelligence and the operation of executive and controlling functions.

An example of an afferent system is the process of statistical returns operated in hospitals in England and Wales. Each provides a monthly return of bed numbers, staff numbers and types, and bed-occupancies in different divisions. The results are assembled at regional headquarters, and the regional statistics are assembled nationally. The main purpose of the system is to assist in medium/long-term financial planning. These processes, which are purely of an afferent nature, are carried out by clerks, and epidemiologists are not involved. Apart from the (eventual) publication of aggregated data the individual hospitals receive no direct service based upon the returns. Purely afferent systems of this kind are often of limited value because of difficulties in maintaining quality. In general, the quality of data is improved if the contributors to the afferent component of a system derive direct and immediate benefits from their contribution.

Drug prescriptions provide a ubiquitous example of an efferent process. When a doctor writes a prescription for a drug he may be considered as a component of a health care information system, and his prescription is an output. The prescription then becomes an *instrument*, through which the drug is delivered. However, in countries with central payment for drugs the document then becomes an 'input' which, after aggregation with other prescriptions, is used to generate payment (another output) to the pharmacist. Aggregated inputs may be used for economic analysis, or for general monitoring. They may also be used to check upon irresponsible or overexpensive prescribing on the part of practitioners and a further 'output' is directed to appropriate disciplinary authorities. Thus, the prescription, which is an efferent component of the sub-system for treating a patient, becomes an afferent component in two other sub-systems, one fiscal, and the other concerned with quality control.

Information processes have sometimes been classified on the basis of being 'scientific' or 'operational'. In the field of automated processing this has been reflected in the development of separate families of computer languages for 'scientific' and 'commercial' operations. The afferent and efferent examples given above would, under the terms of this taxonomy, be regarded as 'commercial'. 'Scientific' processes would from this point of view be regarded as entirely data-acquisitive and analytical, the analytical methods covering both data-reduction (e.g. statistical) processes, and model-building and model-fitting activities. Unfortunately, the scientific/ operational dichotomy has led in the past to the separation of professional activities which ought to have been integrated, and to difficulties in building appropriate scientific inputs and scientific control into service experiments and evaluative innovations.

For these reasons we suggest that a more appropriate dichotomy would be one which divides information processes on the criterion of formality, or explicitness. That is, we recognize:

(a) Those processes which are formal, and follow explicit rules, and which are consequently verifiable in the sense that their outcomes may be described as 'right' or 'wrong'.

(b) Those which do not follow formal rules and which, consequently, are not verifiable. These activities may be based upon previous tacit knowledge, or be derived from intuitive mental processes, or a combination of the two. In the absence of formal verification the main criterion of success is 'utility'.

Formal information processes include the use of statistical processes, such as the compilation of 'distributions' from raw data, the calculation of arithmetic means and of indices of dispersion about means, and indices of association or dependency within multi-dimensional distributions. They also include the application of rules for classifying individual events, people, or states into the categories of a previously derived taxonomy. Successful execution requires experience of the problems and techniques of designing and completing questionnaires and taking measurements. Each of these operations can be defined in formal terms as a set of rules of procedure. Straightforward rules may be laid down for identifying individual records, for linking records from different files, for assembling new elements within an existing record, or new records within an existing file, and for authorizing each of these operations.

The definition of a correct procedure is dependent upon precise definition of the object on which the operation is performed and of the structure within which the object is located, which in this case includes elements, records, files, reports, etc. An intuitive understanding of these structures and their relationships may be sufficient where most of the processes are carried out by human beings, but where computers are made to do the work quite intricate syntactic definitions may be needed.

In contrast with exactly definable operations of these kinds, there is a set of non-formal information processes which are governed less by the notion of 'correctness' than by the notion of utility. Examples of these non-formal processes include the choice of the universe from which a sample is to be drawn and, once that choice has been made, the selection of an appropriate sampling procedure. Others are the choice of the most appropriate taxonomy for classifying states or events or individuals, the construction of biological and behavioural models to 'explain' patterns of observations, the identification of the appropriate audience for a report and the design of the presentation in a form which the audience can readily interpret, the design of service experiments and judgements on their ethics, and assessments of the degree to which a hypothesis can be considered proven.

The formal and non-formal aspects of information processes are mutually dependent and mutually interactive. The distinction between them does not correspond to any sectorization of the way in which an information system is managed. That is, there is no basis for segregating the formal activities as the sole responsibility of workers with particular technical skills (e.g. statisticians), while retaining the non-formal processes entirely for those without them (e.g. clinicians). It should be evident, also, that the distinction between and the interplay of formal and non-formal processes apply equally to those areas of work which traditionally belong to administrators and to those which traditionally belong to scientists.

Any differences between these traditional roles are best seen as differences of emphasis. The tenets of rational planning demand that *someone* should be skilled and experienced in both kinds of activity whether this be an experienced statistician with adequate clinical or biological knowledge, or a clinician with an understanding of handling data, or an epidemiologist.

7.4. SYSTEMS

In §§ 7.1 and 7.2 we described the ways in which the elements of health care information as interrelated, both in structural and in process terms. In Chapters 8 and 9, we shall describe the ways in which elements and assemblies of health care information are related to the outside world. These descriptions, taken together, meet the general definition of an open 'system', as given in Chapter 2.

The conceptual unity of structure, content, meaning, process, and application have been strongly reinforced in recent years by the advent of computer-based automatic data processing techniques. Part of the effect was physical; that is, expensive and powerful equipment and rare and highly paid skills enforced the concentration of activities within specialized units. A more important effect, however, arose from the improved scientific and philosophical understanding of information processes which these new techniques engendered. This improved understanding may be seen as centred on the concept of an algorithm, which is the formal means of expressing a data-handling operation. Crudely stated, it is an algebraic expression written in the imperative mood, saying what is to be done rather than (as in an equation) what is. In such expressions the elements of information which are to be manipulated are called *operands* and the symbols representing the ways in which they are to be manipulated are called *operators*. Expressions and sequences of expressions containing both *operands* and *operators* constitute algorithms, and algorithms, written to appropriate grammatical rules and arranged in proper sequence, become computer programmes.

The use of computers made it necessary, in handling information, to identify the different types of *operands* (e.g. value-types), and to assign an *operator* appropriate to that type of *operand* but not to another. This discipline led to a greater clarity of understanding of information structures in general, of practical operations, of the rules of procedure whereby false arguments may be recognized, and of the mechanisms through which desired results may be obtained. The basic operations of computer programming reflect the non-computer operations traditionally performed upon items of medical and health information. They include reading, writing, copying, adding, sub-tracting, dividing, multiplying, comparing, and many others. Declarations of the truth or falsity of propositions (e.g. diagnoses) are also catered for in computing languages; they are termed 'boolean' or 'logical' values. Even the 'instrumental' form of information, as exemplified in a prescription, has its formal mode of expression; it is recognized as an information element of type 'procedure'. The 'algorithmic' languages provide a representational correspondence between all the information manipulations carried out by people and those carried out by machine, and a unified conceptual system for understanding the structure, the components, and all the formal operations of health care information.

8. The uses of information in health care planning

In this section we are concerned with information in the sense of 'intelligence'. That is, we suppose that most of the mechanical and analytical processing has been completed and that we wish to identify planning outlets. Any taxonomy which we impose upon the system, here, will be related to its uses rather than (as in Chapter 7) its processing and management. Even so, there are several alternative ways of classifying the components of intelligence.

A first taxonomy might relate to the three main elements of the balancing equation with which planners are necessarily concerned. These relate to (i) need (or demand), (ii) resources, and (iii) standards. Since planning is usually incremental and concerned with improvements over an existing situation, we might add a block of information relating to existing activities and existing deployments of service resources. And since planning is based upon projections as well as facts, we shall require demographic and other information necessary for making forecasts and for identifying constraints upon freedom of action.

A second taxonomy would relate to the administrative level at which the planning was envisaged. Health care planning at the level of a group practice or a surgical unit has different information requirements from planning at the level of a hospital or at the level of a total service, and planning in relation to any of these institutions has different requirements from planning in relation to functionally defined services as described in § 4.2. These different contexts require different sources, different forms 'of presentation, and different distributions of result.

A third taxonomy relates items of information to the specificity of purpose for which they are envisaged. At one extreme we have routinely collected information provided for quite general purposes such as describing the background picture or for monitoring a general level of service performance. Next, there are intermittently applied enquiries such as censuses and, more specifically still, a range of special purpose-directed scientific studies, and commissions of enquiry with political objectives. Some sets of data are collected routinely for one purpose (e.g. payments), but used opportunistically for others. Some systems change their initial purposes; others appear never to have had any at all or, in time, to have lost any purposes which they once may have had.

It may be recognized that the structure of health care intelligence follows the pattern of a matrix structure as described in Chapter 4, § 2. This is not inappropriate, since health care systems—which the information system represents—are themselves structured in this way. We shall not, therefore, in the following sections attempt to force our discussion into any one of the alternative patterns, but will comment on aspects of information relevant to each of them.

8.2. INFORMATION FOR ASSESSING NEED

Medical need may be defined in such terms as 'some disturbance in health and well-being' which requires medical care services (Donabedian 1973). However, qualitative definitions of need have only a limited use in health care planning contexts and they hide, or fail to answer, several important questions. First, the planner is necessarily concerned with the future, and with estimates of continued need, rather than (simply) its existence. Second, especially at higher levels of allocating central resources he must be concerned with the notion of 'group' needs rather than (only) those of individuals, and with quantitative rather than qualitative issues. Finally, he must be aware that need is always a perception and that its assessment depends upon whose perception it is. The patient's perception is not necessarily that of the doctor whom he consults and, indeed, they may be in frank conflict. The different components of need perceived by a patient may be incompatible with each other as may (less frequently we hope) the components perceived by the doctor. Another perception of need is that which emerges in discussion between the physician and his client and this is the basis of the advice which the physician gives concerning whether and how the need should be met. In the case of preventive procedures the perception of need may be generated almost entirely by the physician. In the case of acute episodes it may be decided almost entirely by the patient (e.g. toothache, injuries). In other instances (e.g. a patient who falls unconscious in the street) it may be determined almost entirely by a third party.

Epidemiologists and others who study populations frequently find that a far larger proportion of disease is hidden from view than is evident to administrators, physicians, or to the general public. The analogy of an iceberg, only the tip of which is seen, is widely used. The term 'unperceived need' is applied to disease which is recognized neither by its victim nor by his medical attendants. Where the size of the problem is known, but the affected individuals unidentified, assessment of 'need' may be applied to groups, and these assessments are greater than the aggregate of individual perceptions. For preventive purposes, need may also be perceived in terms of the presence of a *risk* of disease, or in terms of exposure to hazard (e.g. cigarette smoking), and since not all those exposed will suffer, this also invokes the notion of a 'group' need.

Whether at the individual or at the group level, the concept of need is linked with the possibility of effective action. The condition with no effective cure or relief, or which is likely to resolve spontaneously, does not constitute a need in the same urgent sense as a disease for which an effective treatment is both necessary and available (e.g. appendicitis), and, where a useful treatment becomes available where previously there was none, need is actually created (e.g. arthroplasty for osteo-arthritis of the hip).

So far as the *measurement* of need is concerned, the perceptual and interactive nature of the concept creates a difficulty. We cannot easily conceive of a bank of information of objective needs, but only of the factual data on which current and future perceptions might be based. It does not help us if we try to differentiate between need and demand. The connotation of the latter term is simply that the need has been expressed by the person who perceived it, and it might depend upon assessments with which another person would not agree; this would then be classified as an 'unjustified demand'. The notion of 'met demand' is more concrete but is an unnecessary circumlocution, being simply a statement of service provided. The relationship between the notion of need and the provision of effective care depends essentially upon the *possibility* of providing that care, rather than its actual provision. These lines of thinking have been developed by Matthew (1971) and Glass (1976) who see need as only being identifiable where there is available 'some medical intervention that has positive utility and that actually alters the prognosis of the disease in some favourable way at reasonable cost'. Glass (1976) insists that 'need' should not be used for planning unless it can 'be determined by measurable qualities against agreed standards' and implies that the establishment of these standards is not the responsibility of any single professional group.

8.3. INFORMATION FOR CONTROLLING UTILIZATION AND STANDARDS

Unlike need, whose assessment depends chiefly upon information acquired from the population at large, information about health service activities and utilization is derived from the records of the health care service itself. Where health services are readily accessible reasonable people will demand and use the services they require and the usage provides an index of need, but where access is restricted, or the service inequitably distributed, this does not hold. Alderson (1975) also points out that the completion of a consultation is not itself proof that a need has been met; the episode must be accompanied by (appropriate) patient satisfaction.

Waiting lists serve as one index of currently unmet demand, but they require cautious interpretation. In some instances the waiting time may have been deliberately planned for social or medical reasons and sometimes patients are on more than one waiting list. Where the latter practice has been adopted many patients on a given list may have already been dealt with through an alternative arrangement. In some cases it is only the existence of a long list (e.g. for tonsillectomy) which encourages a physician to recommend the entry of a patient's name, knowing that spontaneous resolution may occur during the circuitously planned period of 'observation'. Finally, it has not been unknown for physicians to use waiting lists as a basis for emphasizing the demand for services, or the shortfall of resources provided. The simple length of a waiting list is not in itself an indication of discrepancy between demand and supply, and it may be more important to study the distributions of sojourn upon waiting lists of samples of patients eventually treated, and, since the picture may be different, upon samples chosen prospectively from the point of entry. When supplemented by studies of these kinds, waiting list dynamics can indeed provide valid indices of need for change, especially in situations where the service to be provided is reasonably well validated and accepted. Examples are waiting lists for the treatment of strabismus, cataract, inguinal hernia, procidentia, and so on. For conditions where the decision to recommend treatment is more arbitrary the position is correspondingly more difficult: for example for tonsillectomy, haemorrhoids, hysterectomy for metrorrhagia, and treatment for varicose veins. To begin with, repeated assessments on different occasions or by different observers characteristically reveal a lack of complete correspondence in the assessment of need for an operation at all. In the second place, where there is a system of referral from general practitioners to hospitals, the known existence of long waiting lists and of prolonged waiting times, will encourage practitioners to shift their necessarily arbitrary criteria for referral, and this may be reflected to some extent in changes in the patients' own criteria for seeking advice from the general practitioners.

Studies of the activity distributions of health care units, especially when seen in relation to waiting lists, can provide indications of the balances between supply and demand and of the ways in which overriding priorities force out the lesser priorities in situations where resources are inadequate. Thus, the activities of a general surgical unit may indicate high frequencies of exploratory laparotomies and surgery for acute abdominal emergencies against non-existing waiting lists for these conditions. Inguinal hernia may have a substantial waiting list, but one which is characterized by frequent additions at one end, frequent exits to surgery at the other end, and only a moderate average waiting time. Further down the list of priorities there may be a long and growing waiting list for treatment of haemorrhoids, and infrequent admissions.

However, the main general uses of activity analysis (hospital activity analysis, general practice activity analysis, laboratory activity analysis) are in relation for 'self appraisal' and 'peer review' activities on the parts of the practitioners themselves. These activities are essentially private, and therefore not threatening; they are also for this reason acceptable, especially in units which already have high standards. Their drawbacks are that they may lack credibility just because of their privacy, that they tend not to be carried out in units whose standards are such as to indicate particular need for them, and that they are not usually related to outcomes. Nevertheless there is little doubt that they are valuable as educative exercises and may raise standards, provided that the results are presented before they are out of date and in a manner which is relevant to the internal management problems of the units concerned. The raising of standards depends as much upon a secondary analysis of clinical records as upon statistical presentations. High rates of burst abdomen, of wound infection, of unnecessarily prolonged admission, and low rates of investigations generally deemed necessary (rectal examination, haemoglobin estimation) are detected in discussion and often corrected; fresh standards may be laid down and the future quality of the service set against them. Because of the (usual) absence of output criteria, or of definitions of standards other than those set by the practitioners themselves, and the absence of an overview of the total service—as opposed to the localized service provided by the unit—activity analysis should seldom be regarded as a sufficient evaluation of a service—although certainly a necessary one.

8.4. INFORMATION FOR CONTROLLING THE DEPLOYMENT OF RESOURCES

The physical resources for a health care system can be divided into several broad categories; human, financial, buildings, equipment, etc. It is necessary to have information about the current 'stock' of each of them, about their geographical deployments, and their activities or use. It is desirable, if possible, to assemble knowledge about their effectiveness in relation to the tasks undertaken and to ascertain the effects of deficient provision. It is also important, for each, to maintain projections of likely supply, set against projections of likely demand, and to identify important constraints upon freedom of redeployment, as far in advance as is possible.

Manpower is the most important resource in a labour-intensive industry such as health care. It absorbs a large proportion of any health care budget, partly because some personnel (e.g. physicians, surgeons, senior administrators) may be highly paid by national standards, but mainly because of the very large numbers of moderately paid staff (e.g. nurses, technicians, ancillaries) which the service employs.

Rational manpower planning for each class of personnel requires information on (a) the current stock of trained persons, both active and inactive, (b) the prospective supply (including those under-going training and immigrants), and (c) prospective losses (retirements, deaths, emigrants). Some of these requirements will be met by information gathered within the health care service itself, but infor-mation from outside will also be needed. Hall and Mejia (1978) in a consideration of these information problems indicate the importance of training arrangements and the feasibility of government inter-vention in the control of recruitment and deployment. With respect to deployment, the possibility of influencing the geographical distribution of doctors may be a major consideration, especially between urban and rural areas. Such problems will differ for different manpower classes and the siting of health care facilities may be determined by a need for compromise. It may be difficult to obtain doctors for a small hospital some distance from large cities, while there may be a ready supply of women with nursing experience close to its proposed site, who would not be prepared to travel to larger urban centres.

Problems of manpower supply depend on whether recruitment and training programmes are arranged within the health care system itself as is the case, usually, with nurses and laboratory technicians, or whether the responsibilities lie elsewhere, as is usual for doctors and other scientific staff. The scale on which the supply operation takes place (e.g. national) is typically larger than that at which demand forecasting is crucial (e.g. regional). For doctors especially, although also for other types of personnel, international migration has removed supply planning from any effective control so far as many countries are concerned. Even ascertainment is difficult, as shown by the WHO Multinational Study on the International Migration of Physicians and Nurses (1978). Hall has indicated three main sources of manpower data, namely:

(a) *Official sources* (e.g. licensure boards, legally sanctioned professional registries, tax offices, official statistical bulletins on health resources and resource use, payroll and personnel records).

(b) *Non-official institutional sources* (e.g. membership rolls of professional societies, personnel and statistical records of private hospitals and other institutions, lists of practitioners qualified to receive reimbursement from insurance companies, telephone directories, lists of practitioners prepared by pharmaceutical companies);

(c) *Primary field data sources* (surveys of individuals by mail, telephone, or personal interview, etc.)

Data collection alone is not sufficient for manpower planning purposes and predictive and extrapolative studies are required. Large-scale complex services with high levels of professional differentiation and specialization, and with complex specialist training pathways, require projections which are beyond reliable intuitive management. In recent years there has been a substantial development of medical manpower simulators, using computers, and there is no doubt that they will be increasingly used. Projections of these kinds, however effective, do not of course answer the burning question as to how many doctors will be needed. The demand for health care resources is always elastic and responds in some degree to the supply. Doctors and nurses will probably always be employed up to limits imposed by economic or political considerations or both. Where there is comprehensive planning of medical manpower the decision, more and more, will be a political one. That is, it will reduce essentially to the question of how much the community is prepared to pay for its health care services, and the outcome will depend with increasing clarity upon negotiations between the representatives of the health professions and the representatives of their clients.

Information necessary or available for planning financial investments in health care services varies in different economies. Sometimes all funds will be derived from a single national budget but more frequently will come from several sources. In the latter event it may not be possible to ascertain all sources with accuracy and to construct a comprehensive accounting system. The task is simplified when most of the resources come from public sources, whether governmentally organized or through insurance schemes or occupational groups, and the most difficult to deal with are those which occur at a purely private and individual level. Opportunities for effective planning will be limited in this last situation but for the planner faced with this situation the task is no less difficult.

In a study carried out in Colombia, a simple approach was used to identify sources of health expenditures. Public, private, and other sources were distinguished, the relevant agencies were identified, and each was cross-classified by the type of health service it provided. The accounting systems from which the information was given were not primarily suited to the purposes of the authors and a number of adaptations were necessary. In effect, the investigators had to define the limits of the 'health sector' and to devise the principles and criteria for inclusion or exclusion of expenditures. They included funds provided for all activities exerting a direct impact on health, encompassing preventive and curative activities, the training of health personnel, the construction and equipping of health care facilities, and medical research. It was also necessary to ensure that inputs at every administrative level (national, departmental, municipal) in the country were taken into account, that they referred to the appropriate period of time, and that no item of expenditure was counted more than once, whether it originated in a health agency or elsewhere. The sources included the government, via several agencies including the ministries of health, education, public works, defence, and others; also regional and municipal sources, charities, industries and voluntary agencies, international agencies, and the private sector. It was not possible to be accurate in respect of every input/output combination but reasonable estimates could be made where accurate information was not available. Where possible, information on a given expenditure was obtained from different sources, and any discrepancies had to be reconciled (Colombia, Ministry of Public Health and Colombian Association of Medical Schools 1967).

Information for planning the provision, distribution, effectiveness, and state of maintenance of building and equipment may, like financial resources, be obtained from many sources. In countries with comprehensive national health services this kind of information is usually collected routinely by central government (although it may be of doubtful or varying quality) and statistical breakdowns are usually provided. In other countries, the licensing, registration, and inspection arrangements provide similar data. In less developed situations data may come from occasional censuses, or central contributions to local budgets, and records of new buildings and acquisitions; the total picture is then likely to be incomplete and of limited accuracy and, in particular, to be out of date. Nevertheless, with ingenuity and application, a competent and adequate intelligence network can often be established. The Ministry of Health and the Association of Medical Schools of Colombia (Colombia, Ministry of Public Health 1972) compiled and made available a list of names and addresses of all health facilities or establishments in the country. They include health centres, health posts, hospitals, etc. stratified by size, type, ownership, and current activity level. More recently this has been elaborated and supplemented by a series of specific surveys, the latest of which reported on the current status of electromedical equipment, commodities, supplies, and physical plant. On the basis of this work a national project for the maintenance of hospital equipment is being implemented.

8.5. INFORMATION FOR ENHANCING THE EFFECTIVENESS OF SERVICES

The information uses referred to above are related to planning the supply of services and to the standards of provision. That is, they are directed towards input planning. There is little in these sections related to the assessment and enhancement of the efficacy of the component procedures of the service, or to the effectiveness of the services as a whole when measured in terms of true outputs. Responsibilities for providing and analysing information directed to these purposes are largely scientific and characteristically, although not solely, the province of the epidemiologist.

This is far from a straightforward task. Apart from the technical problems of collecting and validating data on the activities and outcomes of a complex set of service functions, there are serious inductive difficulties. One of the most difficult problems is that of separating in any quantitative sense the effects of the health care service itself from the confounding effects of changes in the larger environment. Declines in the incidence and mortality of tuberculosis have been observed in many parts of the world and the health care services can justifiably claim that antibiotics, isolation, contact tracing, and BCG vaccination must have played their parts. Nevertheless, mortality and incidence were in many places declining before these measures were introduced, and the times when they were introduced are not self-evident from the morbidity and mortality trends themselves. The introduction of prophylactic measures for the control of haemolytic disease of the newborn due to rhesus iso-immunization provides another instance of this kind of difficulty. Incidence and mortality were simultaneously affected by demographic changes in family size distributions—the disease being more frequent in later births—and by changing availabilities of pregnancy termination and of selective sterilization. Cancer registries provide another example; most of them were set up in the first place with a view to monitoring the effectiveness of care, yet few have succeeded in doing so. They have been far more successful in demonstrating 'spontaneous' changes in incidence and mortality and the geographical variations which most of the cancers exhibit.

A further complication is that the information-ascertainment techniques employed, themselves influence the apparent morbidity pattern. Thus, introductions of hypertension screening or of cervical-cancer screening themselves stimulate an apparent rise in incidence and prevalence. Similarly, a rise in the notifications of dysentery will itself stimulate the medical attendants of patients suffering from gastro-enteritis to conduct bacteriological examinations, and this may 'cause' an explosive epidemic. Changes in diagnostic fashions, among clinicians, tend to produce longer term effects. Increasing awareness of ischaemic heart disease syndromes during this century is in part responsible for this modern epidemic. Changing thresholds for the attachment of such diagnoses can modify the severity and prognosis of the disease, as it was previously understood, and this provides another problem for those who wish to evaluate the performance of the treatment services. A modern facet of this problem arises out of the increasing provision, and therefore the increasing ease of admission, to intensive care units.

The most successful demonstrations of health care service effectiveness have been in relation to well-defined pathological conditions where comprehensive provision of care has demanded the construction and maintenance of special information services. Examples include the detection and treatment of phenylketonuria, congenital dislocation of the hip, haemolytic disease of the newborn, chorion-epithelioma, vaccination and immunization services, tuberculosis and venereal disease contact-tracing services, and a few mass treatment campaigns (e.g. yaws). There are also several examples where the harmful effects of health care provision have been clearly demonstrated through drug monitoring, radiation monitoring, or the notification of malformations. Unfortunately, the conditions for which effective assessments have become available through routine information collecting, or through information systems necessary for the delivery of the service, constitute only a small minority of the problems with which most modern health care systems are faced, and a comprehensive approach demands the design and execution of a large number of special enquiries.

A major conceptual distinction is drawn, in health care enquiries, between those based upon experimental and non-experimental techniques. An experiment may be defined as an enquiry based upon a manipulation, its purpose being to find out the effect of the manipulation. The design of the experiment is based upon a hypothesis of 'cause', and the outcome has direct implications for subsequent action. Non-experimental enquiries and surveys, by contrast, permit less direct and less specific interpretation.

In practice, experimental designs are more readily applied to testing the efficacy of procedures rather than measuring the effectiveness of total health care systems. This applies both to experiments designed in the format of the randomized controlled trial (e.g. Cochrane 1972), and those consisting of sequential studies of individuals in the format customarily used by experimental pathologists. In both instances the exigencies of health care planning require an act of extrapolation from the circumstances of the experiment to the circumstances of the service; that is, a transfer of conclusion from one geographical location to another, from one period of time to another, or to circumstances in which modified doses or modified regimes are to be used. These requirements arise, in the main, from the extreme specificity of the questions which exact experiments ask and answer. It is also for this reason that there is a broad requirement for non-experimental survey work; despite the problems of exact interpretation which arise in the non-experimental situation, such studies provide the terrain contours against which the spot estimates of the experimenter can be placed.

An enlarged consideration of the field and analytical techniques appropriate to this area of work is provided in Part III of this book.

9. Sources of information

9.1. INTERNAL AND EXTERNAL SOURCES

We saw in Chapter 8 that information marshalled for the purposes of planning health care services is obtained from many sources. Information for controlling the resources and activities of a service is obtained very largely through its own supporting information system, but assessments of need and effectiveness depend upon access to external data sources. A great deal of this information is collected in support of civil authorities, social services, educational services, and industrial planning. It is not surprising, therefore, that much of it is inadequate for health planning purposes, and requires supplementation through special surveys and studies. In the following sections we shall consider information derived from the more important external and internal sources, and the necessary supplementary activities.

9.2. DEMOGRAPHIC SOURCES

The population census was first used in China, in A.D.754, and modern censuses have a history of about 200 years. Their purpose is the enumeration of the whole population at a defined point of time and within defined geographical boundaries and the process involves tracing, identifying, recording, processing, and publishing. Special legislation is normally required to make participation obligatory and to give authority to the organizers.

A successful census is a difficult large-scale operation and the quality and reliability of the result depend upon the success with which it is planned and executed. There are numerous examples of unsuccessful attempts at enumeration, producing data so untrustworthy as to be practically useless. One serious difficulty in many parts of the world relates to personal identification. The first-name/surname system of identification—developed usually for military and taxation purposes in medieval times—is not used in all countries, and even this system gives rise to ambiguities in large modern populations. The use of unique identifying numbers for such purposes as taxation, insurance, or electoral management is quite rare. Although the construction of population registers containing identities is not a prime purpose of a census, the absence of an accurate means of personal identification is a major hindrance. If, as in some cases, the census operation is also used in order to construct population registers on which taxation (for example) could be based, it provides strong incentives to avoid participation. Recommendations about censuses have been laid down in 1960 and 1970 by the World Census Programme. (For example, see U.N. Statistical Office 1965, 1967.)

In addition to gross enumeration, most censuses attempt to construct age and sex distributions. Again, there may sometimes be problems where ages are not accurately known. Many censuses collect other information in addition, either from the whole population or from samples. This information may relate to occupation, country of birth, languages spoken, fertility, or recent migration patterns. In some countries, where a complete decennial census is taken, annual sample surveys are conducted between the two censuses in order to monitor demographic changes and to undertake special studies.

There are other, although less satisfactory, ways of estimating population sizes and structures in societies without facilities for conducting censuses, mainly through sampling procedures. The samples may be based upon occupational groups, electoral registers, educational facilities, or aerial photography for the identification of dwellings. Each has its uses and its defects but all these techniques are most suitably used as supplements to censuses rather than as substitutes.

Registrations of births and deaths, where they are available, provide another means of keeping census data up to date. Birth and death registrations have great value for health planners even when censuses are not available, particularly when age and sex and cause of death are also recorded. Records of these kinds are a first priority in any country which lacks adequate information on health care needs. In more advanced societies, registration of the fact and the cause of stillbirth is another valuable acquisition. Registration of births and deaths, together with registrations of marriages, are commonly carried out through civil authorities and published by them, but their value to health care planners is inestimable. The accuracy of assignment of causes to deaths and stillbirths depends upon the type of personnel responsible for recording it. Accuracy also varies from disease to disease and from age group to age group and epidemiologists are well aware of the circumspection necessary in interpreting statistical measures derived from such material.

Epidemiologists and other social scientists commonly use corrected census data as the denominators upon which to base estimates of incidence and prevalence of disease and disability, as ascertained in geographically-bounded populations. Registered deaths, classified according to cause, sex, and age represent one class of the data which may be set upon such denominators.

The age/sex structures of populations themselves provide the health planner with a means of estimating certain gross needs. For example, many rural tropical societies display very high proportions of children, an age structure which usually reflects high early mortalities. In certain geographical areas of western countries—so called 'retirement' areas—there may be very large numbers of elderly people. The special preventive, therapeutic, and supportive services required by such societies can often be guessed with a fair degree of accuracy on the basis of these data alone, assisted perhaps by extrapolation from neighbouring societies with somewhat different population structures.

Information on migration is also necessary both to the investigator and the planner. For the former it is important to know the rate of interchange between a studied society and its neighbouring societies if calculations of incidence and prevalence are to be made accurately. Counting the entrants to a cervical-cytology screening scheme may soon appear to demonstrate that well over 100 per cent of the eligible women have been accessed, if appropriate corrections are not made to allow for new and unregistered women entering the area, and the departure of many of those already registered. For the planner it is especially important when immigrants come from areas with different health problems or are of different racial groups. In Britain, for example, large-scale immigration of families of Asian and African origin tends to make nonsense of routinely applied screening for phenylketonuria—the incidence in these families is low—and at the same time raises a requirement for selective screening for haemoglobinopathies.

Demographic *projection* is necessary for longer-term planning of health services. Rising or falling fertilities have immediate implications for the provision of maternity services and somewhat longer-term implications with respect to paediatric and school health services and, ultimately, occupational and general health services. Oscillations in birth rates are reflected in secondary oscillations in total numbers of births, although not necessarily rates, when the primary wave moves through to the reproductive age period. It is important to try to discern whether a reduction in birth rate such as has occurred in recent years in many western countries, represents a permanent or persistent alteration of behaviour, or whether economic circumstances and the improved availability of contraceptives has induced women simply to postpone having their families; in this case a short-term increase in births might be expected. In the longer term these various trends and oscillations are reflected in requirements for geriatric services, both medical and social. Population changes also have important implications with respect to health care resources, through influencing the general economic status of the country and the ratio between producers and dependants, but also in such matters as the availability of women for nursing.

9.3. OTHER NON-MEDICAL SOURCES OF INFORMATION

The main non-demographic information sources outside the health care services themselves, relate to the provision of personal social services, social security and sickness insurance, nutrition, occupation, economics, and the control of the environment. There are two main ways in which these sources can help the health care planner. The first relates to the direct provision of statistical descriptive material, and the second is through a capacity to provide samples for purposes of conducting special enquiries. For the latter it is possible to use sources which do not necessarily provide direct statistics at all, for example electoral registers, driving licence registers, and others.

The contents of such registers and the methods of compiling and maintaining them vary markedly between different nations, although the UN Population Commission has recommended standardized practices. These recommendations are based upon the supposition that apart from meeting their primary purposes, registers should be designed to provide a basis for research in such fields as public health, medicine, and social welfare. Working definitions have been provided of the various life events with which demographers are concerned and of the details which should be collected in respect of each event. A detailed tabulation programme has also been drafted which, since 1948, has been published by the United Nations Organization in its annual *Demographic Year-book.*

Some nations maintain comprehensive and continuous registration systems. They comprise the personal records of every member of the population; each is continuously kept up to date in respect of such simple facts as abode, occupation, and civil status. With the development of modern 'databank' systems with individual identification numbers, the maintenance of a fully comprehensive central store may be unnecessary. A central population register with basic descriptive and identification data may be supplemented as necessary by linking it with socio-economic or health information from other registers. As the technical difficulties of such linkage operations are overcome, more countries are finding it possible to link social security registers with national population registers. Although continuous registration systems are functioning successfully in some smaller European nations the possibility of abusing the confidential material contained in personal records has made such systems unpopular with the public elsewhere. The imaginative combination of a register of basic demographic events with retrospective surveys based on sickness occurrence and information from other registers or from censuses offers potentialities for the longitudinal analysis of many health problems. For some purposes it is sufficient to limit these continuous registration systems to sub-samples of the population. Such a system has been functioning in Sweden since the census of 1950 with respect to individuals with a birthday on the fifteenth of any month, and specially collected data have been used for a number of different purposes for example fertility analyses (Bernhardt 1971).

Despite the potential value of general population registers, most countries obtain their statistical social information from other sources, partly demographic, partly from special purpose registers, and partly from data collected in the course of managing a variety of social sub-systems. Information of these kinds is exceedingly important to planners of health and health care services; these services are, in the language of systems theory, 'open systems', in that they interact extensively with the social and physical environment within which they operate. In many countries the main task of the epidemiologist and social scientist is to relate these data to the health care system.

No attempt can be made to compile an exhaustive list of such sources but they are frequently available from reports issued by government departments responsible for census, labour, industry, mining, commerce, health and social insurance, environmental protection, agriculture, fisheries, natural resources, etc. In addition there are several international sources, for example the World Health Statistics Annual, the Food and Agriculture Organization, the Organization for Economic Co-operation and Development, and others. There are also many sub-national sources, such as local government, social services organizations, environmental control agencies, housing and town planning authorities, highways and transport authorities, bodies responsible for planning and organizing water supplies and river basin management, and many others.

Information from these various sources impinges upon health care planning in many different ways. Sometimes it indicates short- or long-term constraints upon development or growth. Limits to the rate of economic growth will limit the absolute total of national resources, and competition for resources in other sectors such as education, housing, and defence will limit the *proportion* of the resource which can be allocated to health care purposes. Typically, the limits will begin to bite at somewhere between seven and ten per cent of Gross National Product although, in many countries, very much less than this is spent. Rapid changes in the growth of local populations, and those shifts of local age-distributions which make rapid growth likely, also provide longer-term warnings for health care planners. In some cases it is possible to see that there are critical constraints to the local population growth rate; for example, in some cities, the limited possibilities of drainage through a small river, and the difficulty of disposing of sewage, may set an upper bound. Elsewhere, the decline of a major industry such as coal-mining or ship-building, on which a region is economically dependent, has a similar effect. Sometimes, as with the mechanization of agriculture it is possible to forecast not only a halt to the growth of the rural population, but a shift in the age distribution and in the health care dependency characteristics, as younger adults migrate elsewhere. Many of the circumstances recorded in general national statistics are themselves determinants of disease, including certain occupations, poor housing, high levels of atmospheric pollution, low *per capita* income, inadequate nutrition, and uncontrolled population growth. Others are indicators of special demand upon institutional services because of difficulties in coping with the problems at home. Examples are overcrowding, absence of running water or sanitation, high migration rates, or unfavourable ratios between elderly and younger people. Sparsity of population brings other kinds of problems.

Bacterial monitoring reports on the control of milk and food supplies, national surveys on nutrition and expenditure, when available, and chemical specifications of the purity, 'hardness', fluoridation, and heavy-metal contents of drinking water are all of obvious interest. Climatic conditions are sometimes relevant and in some countries or regions there are problems with special pollutants (e.g. atmospheric lead from petrol, or high radiation levels). Some industrial hazards (e.g. explosion, massive toxic release, radiation escape), if they have not already triggered pressures to have them separated from large populations, provide a requirement, at least, for contingency planning. There is an increased interest in developing national and international standards in these respects to guide health and health care planners (WHO 1972).

Useful by-products of many social welfare systems, or insurance organizations, are records on illness-related absenteeism in the working population. These records must be interpreted with some care; they seldom cover the entire labour force and they are typically biased by variations in the conditions under which disability payments are made; also by variations in individual thresholds for seeking compensation. These data, however, are widely used by planners to monitor trends in the health status of the working population.

Records from schools provide information about illness-related absenteeism for another selected group, but only a population-based survey can provide a comprehensive picture.

Because medical and other social services should be complementary to each other, health care planners must be fully informed of the social and welfare services in the community. Frequently the availability of disability payments and other sources of income, home care services, physical and occupational therapy, counselling services, and sheltered living and working arrangements, relieve the health care services of those 'caring' functions which, although they are associated with illness and impairment, are not strictly medical. For instance, the presence (or absence) and quality of community-based services that reduce the need for institutionalization, or permit early discharge, are important factors in determining the need for beds in acute care hospitals, nursing homes, and longer-term health care facilities.

9.4. DIAGNOSTIC INDEXES AND REGISTERS

Information sources within the health care system supply inaccurate estimates of need and demand. We saw how reliance upon such material results in an unsatisfactory 'normative' rather than a needs-based approach. Nevertheless there are some exceptions to this general rule and certain kinds of health care information sources can be used with some confidence for estimating total needs. First, there are some diseases and disabilities which almost always come to the notice of the health care system. Indeed, some almost always arrive at a hospital, where they will enter an index and become available for statistical analysis or for further study. Diseases such as leukaemia and acute appendicitis fall into this class. With many other conditions such as Parkinson's disease, cataract, or migraine, the problems of ascertainment are much more difficult. Quantitative estimates of need, based upon measures of 'incidence' have then to be assessed at several different levels of presentation and several different levels of severity. Different results will be obtained at each of these levels.

A second circumstance in which health care data contribute to assessments of need is where doctors or other medical attendants are required by law to notify the date, the place, and the person affected, for a variety of morbid events. They include communicable diseases, in particular, but also certain accidents and industrial diseases and various kinds of disability. Doctors contribute to civil and social information networks through providing assessments of causes of death, of stillbirth, or of absenteeism from school or occupation. Their main contribution to estimating amounts of need in the population may be through such actions. Thirdly, health care systems themselves employ forms of 'internal' notification for certain purposes. Thus, a number of diseases are regularly entered into registers.

Cancer registers, psychiatric registers, and physical disability registers are quite widely used. According to definitions developed by a WHO expert committee (Brooke 1974), 'registration' carries an implication of a permanent record which includes personal identification, and an understanding that further action such as follow-up, is intended. Thus, survival rates, prognoses, and outcomes can be observed and their rates calculated. There may be little guarantee that all cases are entered into a register, although, for those who are, an accurate assessment of secondary need may be calculable. The same applies to registers collected for non-medical purposes; for example registers of the blind and of the partially-blind are usually constructed for purposes of providing social support rather than medical support, and registers of mental and physical handicap are often orientated primarily towards educational needs.

The maintenance of registers is a difficult and expensive task and small planning agencies may not have the necessary resources. They therefore tend to be national or large regional enterprises although local modifications are possible for the study of special problems. From the investigator's point of view they are especially valuable in providing identifiable samples from which special studies can be mounted. An example is found in the longitudinal studies carried out upon patients on a psychiatric register in the U.K.; the investigators were able to predict the declining demand for psychiatric beds in the 1960s (Tooth and Brooke 1961).

In a very few areas, general registers have been set up in which health, demographic, and service data about the resident population are assembled in a central data bank. Early attempts to achieve this involved special collections of data and were described as population laboratories (Breslow 1965; Kessler and Levin 1970). More recently there has been a development of data-linkage techniques based upon more routine information acquisitions as in the Oxford Record Linkage Study in England (Acheson 1967). General registers could provide planners with the best of all possible worlds, and should be capable of producing incidence and prevalence data that are both patient- and population-specific as well as cover all areas of concern, rather than just selected diseases or risk groups. They are however expensive and, in the absence of universal personal numbering systems, cumbersome. There is also in many countries a degree of public opposition to the idea of comprehensive data banks. An accommodation may develop as record-linkage methods display their capabilities. For instance, it has been shown how multiple admissions of a single patient to the same hospital, or to different hospitals, can be traced (Watts and Acheson 1967; Hobbs *et al.* 1976). Acheson and Fairbairn (1971) were able to estimate the incidence of cardiovascular accidents from existing records without going to the expense of conducting a special study. They did this by linking hospital discharge data to mortality data.

9.5. RECORDS OF ITEMS OF SERVICE

Individual items of service such as consultations, vaccinations, anaesthetics, or operations, are sometimes recorded. The record may include the date, the place, the identity of the provider and of the client, and the type of service. It may be legally required, or supply the basis for paying the provider or reimbursing the user or for claiming travelling or other expenses, or be used for registering accountability for the consumption of materials. Sometimes the record is made for health care control or planning purposes; in vaccination procedures, it serves to maintain a record of the vaccination status of the population, and to trace any complications to particular vaccine batches. In countries where large sections of the population are covered by private or semi-private health insurance schemes, and where health care transactions are itemized, administrative records of insurance agencies provide a practical source of frequency data, for different diseases and services.

As we noted earlier a unit of consumption is not necessarily an index of demand or of need; nor can aggregations of units of consumption be taken as accurate indicators of total morbidity. Strictly, items-of-service measure 'process' in the three part 'structure–process–outcome' framework widely used for evaluating health services (Donabedian 1966). Nevertheless, adaptations relating services to outcome are sometimes possible. A commentary upon the utility of item-of-service information in health care planning is provided in two World Health Organization papers: (WHO 1969, 1971).

Utilization of these different data sources is not without problems. The investigator wishing to use the records for a purpose beyond their original intention will find a lack of uniformity or appropriateness in the definitions, terms, taxonomies, and units of measurement. There are often identification problems, so that it is not possible to link together data from multiple sources. Indeed, at certain administrative levels, identifiers entered on primary records will have been deliberately deleted in order to protect confidentiality. Where referral to original records is necessary it may be difficult to obtain access-permission from physicians and surgeons, especially where investigation is seen as somewhat threatening. Sometimes the name of the physician-in-charge may be regarded as the most confidential item and it may then be difficult even to engineer the first approach. This applies also to information other than item-of-service data, for example in studies of medical manpower attempting to use super-annuation or pension registers.

All these sources of data have to be evaluated and assessed with respect to gaps, biases, and other limitations on their validity. In the United States the characteristics of the Medicare Program and of its data base make it a prime source of information about short-stay or acute-hospital in-patient experience of the population aged 65 and over, but Medicare is useless as a source of information relating to the health care of the labour force. In addition, its coverage of nursing home and other long-stay care, and of ambulatory care, is too limited to provide an adequate picture.

Records of purely clinical activities (as opposed to those designed for administrative purposes) include patient registrations and dis-charges, clinical records, ward and clinical logs and daybooks, operating room schedules, records of prescriptions filled, reports from laboratories, X-ray departments, and other supportive services, immunizations, and many other special procedures and activities. To be useful to an investigator there must usually be an intermediate process in which records are screened, validated, included or excluded according to the terms of investigation, tested for duplication, and, often, linked into sets belonging to individuals. It is only then that they can be classified and aggregated to provide information useful for purposes of management, planning, and evaluation (WHO 1971). In the following sections we discuss these problems in more detail in relation to hospital admission and to ambulatory care.

9.6. HOSPITAL RECORDS

Data about hospital activities are readily available in many countries. The high cost and intensity of hospital services, and the fact that hospitals are seen to function better if they have formal communi-cation systems, encourage this availability. The traditional units of usage given in statistical returns include discharge rates, days of treatment (length of stay), and bed-occupancy rates. The events from which these rates are compiled are not person-specific and special investigations of re-admissions are necessary if this defect is to be repaired. If data on the bed capacity of a hospital are taken into account, the turnover rate of an institution can be calculated, i.e. discharges per year per bed. Since this rate simultaneously reflects the number of patients treated, their length of stay, and bed occupancy rate, it is a useful economic indicator of productivity and intensity of service. On occasions, however, this creates problems. When measures are introduced which increase the intensity of service, such as the introduction of automated laboratory facilities or computer-assisted record keeping, the total revenue costs of running the hospital are increased rather than decreased. Where hospitals are financed from a central source according to criteria which take no account of productivity, the effects of such measures may be in conflict with the economic expectations of the administration.

In hospitals and institutions where patients are retained for long periods of time, discharge data should be supplemented with periodic censuses in order to provide distributions of length of stay and to identify patients in need of special review. This may be a difficult task for two main reasons. First, less attention may have been given to data quality control in long-stay than in short-stay hospitals. Second, standard diagnostic codings are imperfect descriptors of disability and impaired functional status. Supplementary investigations may therefore be needed and without them the patients may be classified simply according to the type of institution (rehabilitation, mentally ill, mentally retarded, geriatric, etc.) and the question of the suitability of the institution for the patients' needs defeated by a circular argument. The need for special studies to determine how such institutions are coping with actual needs and demands has been emphasized by several authors (Acheson *et al.* 1971; Murnaghan 1976; Elder and Acheson 1970).

The need for supplementary studies is not confined to the long-stay institutions. They are required in all parts of the hospital service. Without them the routine statistics based upon discharge data and upon census data cannot provide assessments of need, or demand, or efficacy, or effectiveness. They are relatable simply to administrative efficiency and, as we have seen, there are difficulties even here. As a result, many countries now conduct national sample surveys of hospital discharges, and the usefulness of these data for regional and institutional planning is encouraging some countries to develop total coverage of discharges from short-stay or acute hospitals (Ashley 1972; Murnaghan and White 1971). The most common data elements related to episodes of hospital stay are: dates of admission and discharge, patient identification and demographic descriptors such as civil status, age, etc., identifications of hospital service-unit or ward, primary and secondary diagnoses (coded according to the ICD), and surgical and other major procedures, and the disposal of the patient. In several countries in Europe and in the United States uniform terms, definitions, and classifications have been established for a minimum basic data-set describing hospital discharges (DHEW 1972), and WHO committees have recommended the same approach on an international scale. In Britain the Hospital In-patient Enquiry (HIPE), Hospital Activity Analysis (HAA), and the Mental Health Enquiry (MHE) are sources of such information, as is the Hospital Discharge Survey in the USA, which is based on a probability sample of short-term admissions to acute hospital beds.

9.7. AMBULATORY CARE RECORDS

The problems of acquiring and analysing information concerning ambulatory care services are severe. These problems arise from the variety of settings and of personnel involved, and the high-volume/low-cost/labour-intensive characteristics of the constituent activities. Record keeping is often maintained at a very low standard, although this is not inevitable. In Canada, for example, an item of service must be described before payment is made. In addition there are supplementary sources of information relating to items of service supplied by laboratories, radiological services, physiotherapy services, ambulance services, blood transfusion services, pharmacies, prescription-pricing bureaux, distributors of wheel-chairs and aids for the disabled, manufacturers and suppliers of hearing aids and spectacles, and so on. Each information system is designed for its own needs and often without thought for possible wider uses, and most such systems will be very basic. They may serve, however, as a basis for more detailed enquiry.

The most commonly used unit for measuring activity in hospital out-patient settings or in general practice, is the visit or consultation. Formal record-linkage procedures for connecting these events into patient-identifiable sequences are more difficult and less readily available than for hospital discharge data, except in fee-for-service settings where billing requirements may provide an entry. There are also problems of definition. Although the unit of a 'consultation' is less problem-orientated than might be desired, it is at least reasonably objective. The unit of 'an episode', while more accurately problem-orientated, depends for its interpretation upon the provider and is less suitable for comparative studies between different units or different areas. There are circumstances in which neither the notion of a consultation nor an episode is necessarily useful, particularly where a range of secondary, continuing, and supportive care is undertaken. Although the term 'primary medical care' is frequently used as a synonym for services provided by general practitioners, the provision of 'first-access' care is not their sole function, and they provide a wide range of secondary services of a supportive kind

(Pickles 1939; Fry 1966; Hicks 1976). These problems of definition are now widely recognized and attempts have been made to design better systems of classification for ambulatory care problems than the ICD provides (Hogarth 1975; WONCA 1975).

As with hospital in-patient statistics, analyses based upon measures of activity, unsupported by secondary investigations, provide no commentary upon need, or upon the effectiveness of services, or upon the standard of provision. In the field of ambulatory care, moreover, routine mechanisms for carrying out these secondary investigations are in many part of the world all but non-existent. Exceptions are 'the periodic surveys of general practice conducted in the U.K. (OPCS, 1973), and the new National Ambulatory Medical Care Survey in the United States (DHEW 1975). The latter is based on a continuing probability sample of visits to physicians in office-based practice, which will be extended to out-patient departments and other organized settings; in several of the states, the sample has been enlarged to provide regional as well as national data.

10. Managing information systems

10.1. PROSPECTS OF INTEGRAL MANAGEMENT

In this chapter we consider the ways in which health care information must be managed. For this purpose it is necessary to return to the holistic formulation developed in Chapter 7, in which the distinct ideas of content (i.e. intelligence), and of structure and process (i.e. information engineering), were welded together within the comprehensive concept of a 'system'. The extent to which this holistic image can be translated into realities is a separate question, and one whose answer must reflect the simplicity or the complexity of the health care service which the information system serves. A health care system with rudimentary control and planning may acquire very little information. Those items which *are* assembled—for example financial transactions, staff establishments notification of infectious diseases, and a few special categories of item-of-service— may be processed and used separately, without reference to each other.

However, there has been a general movement towards the unification of health care information services, and this is occurring for three main reasons. The first is a demand for increasingly intricate cross-correlated information, arising from the growing complexity of the health care services themselves, and of the planning operations on which they depend. The second is the growth of technical facilities, especially computers, which have enforced rationalization and centralization of data-handling. The third is the substantial development of technique which followed upon these changes, with clarification of the philosophical/scientific bases of the component activities, and the establishment of a cadre of scientific and technical experts in the field.

10.2. THE HUMAN COMPONENT

The task of managing health care information invokes another dimension. This relates to people. Every health care system involves human beings and depends for its proper functioning upon their performance and their behaviour towards each other. With respect to 'mechanical' performance their most pervading characteristic, possibly, lies in their capacity to make mistakes. Whenever such performance is actually measured it is discovered that people make frequent errors in all data-handling operations, beginning with errors of observation and passing through errors of classification, of identification or measurement, of coding, of spelling, of transmission, of timing, of arithmetic, of matching—and indeed of every conceivable data-handling operation. Error rates are raised further by fatigue, by boredom, and by lack of immediate motivations for accuracy. It is always desirable, whenever it can be arranged, that acquisitive intelligence systems should be linked with short-loop efferent mechanisms providing immediate and obvious benefits to the persons responsible for operating the system. For example, if information about immunization procedures is linked with the mechanism for subsequent recall, then the information gathered is more likely to be accurate than if the outputs are remote, consisting only of (eventual) statistical returns.

It is a characteristic of humanly operated information systems, such as hospital and general practitioner clinical records, that they have become adapted to human error rates through the incorporation of high levels of redundant information. That is, there is more information than is really necessary, and if there is an error of spelling or another ambiguity (i.e. lack of resolution) in a name, the patient can still be identified, or have his identity checked, through the use of his address, his bed number, or his age. If his age is incorrectly or inconsistently reported then it can be checked against his recorded date of birth and his physical appearance. He may have a registration number too, but on the whole the human interpreter will prefer to use more traditional criteria. The redundancy of human information systems is reflected also in the use of names as opposed to the use of numbers; many mis-typings or mis-recordings can be recognized as such by eye and even corrected, but the same cannot be said of numbers. The error-free characteristics of computer transmission, and the use of unique identification numbers for totally unambiguous identification of records, offers scope for improvement, especially in very large populations where the risk of false identification is greater. This is one of the undoubted appeals of computer systems. A number of early ventures ran into trouble, however, through recording only those identifying data which the computer itself required (e.g. 8 digits) and through failing to recognize the redundancy of information required for identification of the *patient* (as opposed to the *record*) in all the circumstances in which such identification is needed. Depending upon the circumstances of the exercise the requirement might be for 50, 100, or 200 characters of identifying information. Even at the simple budgetary level of deciding upon the size of a magnetic storage facility in a computer system, the discrepancies between the human requirement and the machine requirements are sufficient to cause trouble, and indeed, have caused trouble.

After their capacity to create errors, the main 'weakness' of human beings involved in information systems is their capacity to react negatively. They may refuse to supply data for fear of compromising the privacy of health records, whether this be the privacy of patients, or the privacy of doctors, or both. Their behaviours in these respects are expressions of more general social constraints. The transfer of information between doctors, or between doctors and nurses, will probably be less restrained than communication between doctors and social workers, or between doctors and educationists. The same is seen in reverse, and educationists and social workers are more likely to communicate freely with each other, than with doctors. Within a health care system doctors operating at the clinical levels are more likely to communicate freely among themselves than with those involved in administration and planning, especially when the planning function takes place at levels with high political contents, or when the salaries or terms of service of the doctors may be manipulated as a result. The influence of these factors on any health information system is considerable and is always a matter for concern. The structural, functional, and organizational problems which beset managers of health information systems have been reviewed in the fourteenth report of WHO (1971).

Where information systems are manned by a labour force which is organized into trade unions, there may be resistance to certain kinds of rationalization. This occurs when it is feared that automation may reduce the number of jobs, or when it changes relative requirements for different kinds of personnel (perhaps in different unions), or where centralization or re-location of facilities changes the geographical distribution of places of work.

There are several approaches to the amelioration of these problems. Educational programmes provide one way of easing the adjustment of people to each other although the nature of the personal interactions and of the educational programmes vary according to the complexity and breadth of function of the information system. The history of the development of the system is also relevant and, depending on its origins, it may be staffed with people from quite different backgrounds such as natural science, engineering, computer science, operational research, economics, accounting, laboratory science, and so on (Schneider 1976).

The main strength of the human components of information systems relate to non-formal processes, including those which are fundamentally incapable of exact specification, and those which are simply difficult or expensive or beyond the currently available resources of staff and equipment. To a very large extent the necessarily human activities correspond with a range of professional skills encompassing the essential activities of clinical scientists, epidemiologists, managers, economists, social scientists, and others.

There can be no hard and fast rules for the manner in which a health care information system should be organized and manned. Nevertheless, several authors (e.g. Knox *et al.* 1972) have pointed out that for moderately complex systems a series of layers must usually be defined, each with different manning and training requirements. At one extreme there is a broad requirement on the part of all medical, nursing, and other health care practitioners to understand the general purposes of information systems and of the ways in which they impinge upon their own fields. Ideally, this knowledge should be provided during basic training in medical and other professional schools. At the other extreme are those people directly involved in the design, implementation, and maintenance of information systems and they require highly specialized knowledge and skills. In a large and complex system the discrepancy between the sizes of these two classes, and the disparity of technical background, will set up a communications gap, and will require one or more intermediate layers with special responsibilities for the development or application of certain parts of the system, such as immunization schemes, or screening recall arrangements, or the surveillance of the chronic sick, or laboratory quality control. Where a system is undergoing active developments the more specialized layers must accept training responsibilities with respect to the less specialized layers, although this is not to say that education in these matters is to be seen as a one-way traffic.

10.3. QUALITY CONTROL

The efficient management of a health care service depends upon the efficient management of its information systems and upon the mechanisms for their coordination and control. This is true both from the point of view of keeping them working in an efficient manner from day to day and from the point of view of their systematic development and improvement. This is a continuous interactive process. The maintenance of quality, the control of errors, and adaptation of the outputs to their purposes can be accomplished only in close association with those who use the information, and utility and efficiency cannot be sensibly defined except against a background of agreement as to what the users really need and want.

As in other sub-systems of the health care planning process we recognize the characteristic pattern of feedback within a cybernetic cyclical system.

Three levels of quality control have been recognized, namely: (a) operational control; (b) programme control; and (c) social control (Schaefer 1974). Operational control requires the maintenance of agreed standards of quantity, quality and timing of inputs, processing, and outputs which ensure that information is complete, accurate, and available in the right place and at the right time. Departures from these criteria may be regarded in qualitative terms as 'errors' of different kinds or described in quantitative terms. The quantitative approach is often the appropriate one, and specified *degrees* of error or delay may, for certain applications, be accepted or even planned.

At different levels of information management, day-to-day operations are the proper concern of a data-processing manager, a hospital records officer, a librarian, a secretary, or a data technician and, in normal circumstances, the process will continue routinely. If the system fails to work satisfactorily, however, special evaluations will be called for and they can take one of several forms. They range from simple mechanical timetabling reviews, through evaluation of effort, performance, and efficiency as more complex criteria are brought to bear. Judgement is required for all these evaluations and it is important not to insist upon absolute accuracy, timeliness, or completeness, when in fact these criteria compete and where reduced standards in one or more of these respects are sometimes acceptable.

Information 'programme control' is distinguished from 'operational control' in that it extends its criteria of effectiveness to the outside world instead of restricting them to internal standards. Quality is assessed in terms of the relevance of results to the purposes for which they were designed. Ideally, precise agreement should first be reached about the needs and objectives which the system is designed to meet, and the exact specifications laid down relating to the necessary hardware (the physical components) and software (program and procedural components). A complex information system consists of a set of 'application programmes', each related to one of the sub-objectives of the total plan. Nevertheless, the problems of delineating requirements in such exact terms should not be under-estimated. Often the evaluator has to attribute purposes to the system which were not explicitly declared in advance, and may have to assume that certain qualities of outputs are desirable in themselves without being able to measure their impact directly: in other words he makes use of 'surrogate' standards (Schaefer 1974). Sometimes he will have to depend upon criteria which lack real precision, but which are still useful (White 1973). For example, it is often said that health information should be *problem-oriented*; that is it should be focused on the problems that patients and populations present to providers. It should also be *person-related* so that, with due regard for confidentiality, persons can be identified and characterized in terms of socio-demographic indicators. It should be *population-based*, so that there are denominators (which may be enrolled populations or geographically defined populations) which allow demographic standardization, and it should be *period-explicit* and *place-specific*. A final standard of a different order is that a health information system should be *parsimonious*, and only those data should be routinely collected for which there is a definite use envisaged in making decisions.

An important criterion of the adequacy of health care intelligence is 'availability on demand'. This is essentially a question of indexing and of librarianship. It is an important function and often neglected. Intelligence systems and data are often scattered over the hierarchical sub-divisions of the health care service and it is difficult for workers in one area to know what is available in another. This will hinder the opportunistic applications of data to purposes for which they were not originally designed. In many health care systems it would be more profitable to improve the usage of information already available, both from local sources and from such sources as annual statistical reports, registers or data banks, surveys, and *ad hoc* studies, than to increase investment in new and sophisticated information systems.

The 'social' level of quality control envisages evaluations based upon interactions with society beyond those of the first intentions of the planners. The division between programme control and social control is therefore arbitrary and depends upon the comprehensiveness of the initial intentions; social interactions are understood to relate to adjustments and adaptations between the information system and its more distant environment.

On the afferent side the system might hope to absorb (or seek) and have available, a current assessment of values placed by the community on problems which the health care service is expected to solve. Attitudes to contraception or to abortion are typical examples. On the efferent side there are problems of acceptability and response. For example, some early developments in electronic data-processing apparently envisaged an entire replacement of simpler ways of collecting data (e.g. with pen and paper) and it has taken time for the more enthusiastic proponents of the new technique to adopt the circumspection of the more cautious.

Another aspect of the social interaction concerns the communication barriers which still exist between information system developers, the medical and caring professions, health planners, administrators, and even the community served by them. Conflicting role expectations on the parts of different participants can convert an information system designed for the common good into a threat and an imposition, to be frustrated wherever possible. The fact that computers require a disciplined, rigorous, and explicit formulation of the problems upon which they are to work is not necessarily a help in such matters; there are many instances where explicitness is not welcomed. The social evaluation of the workings of an information system, and the social skills necessary for its fruitful development will provide scope for some time to come for the most difficult and the most important exercises of the planner/epidemiologist's task. One special aspect of these problems relates to the maintenance of confidentiality.

10.4. CONFIDENTIALITY

The question of the confidentiality of medical records is of special importance in the design and operation of information systems. It is governed by strong conservative traditions dating from Hippocrates through to such modern statements as the Helsinki and Geneva declarations (Edelstein 1943; Declaration of Geneva 1949; Chadwick and Mann 1950; Declaration of Helsinki 1964). It is also an area in which different highly principled objectives may come into stark conflict. Planners and epidemiologists have to exercise a deep and sympathetic understanding of the ethical principles involved, and a high order of pragmatic skill. They may also have to cope with legal questions, including the formal issue of who 'owns' medical records. Do they belong to the doctor, or to the patient, or to a health authority? Can the meaning of the record be 'owned', or is ownership limited to the medium (e.g. paper) on which the record is made? Who has a legal right of access? Who has a legal right or duty to bar access? Do different rules apply to different parts of a medical record, with differentiation between those items which may be regarded as 'public', such as the patient's name and his address, those parts which contain clinical information supplied by the patient, such as the history and physical phenomena, and those parts which contain the interpretations of the physician, such as the diagnosis? Do these items warrant a different status when combined into a comprehensive whole than when dismembered into unconnectable parts? The answers to these questions differ in different communities, and there is wide variation in the degree to which they can be answered at all. Many situations are governed by incomplete or ambiguous legal formulations, and may be handled obliquely through laws which do not refer directly to the handling of records.

'The law protects a man's person, his property, and his reputation, and intrusion upon privacy which does not infringe on these vested rights, may, nonetheless, be attacked by the indirect invocation of existing remedies, such as exist, for example, in the law relating to trespass and to defamation' (Samuels 1972). In practice it is unusual (Springer 1971) for problems to arise with respect to legal liability if the personal medical records are divulged only to those with an evident legitimate interest, for instance in relation to medical research or as evidence in the courts where, in some countries, the records may not legally be withheld.

In practice there is a wide breach of strict confidentiality and the number of people and agencies with legitimate interests in medical information has multiplied in recent years. Many millions are covered by health insurance schemes, there has been a large expansion of governmental participation in health care planning and delivery, and the development of substantial health care teams has required 'shared confidentiality'. This has developed in the main without explicit formulation of its terms so that the subject is clouded by misunderstandings and doubts, despite the fact that it has reached positions from which it would be difficult or impossible to withdraw. The problem becomes particularly acute when it is feared that personal health data may be passed on to governmental agencies. Difficulties may also arise when proposals are advanced for record-linkage, or pooling of data from different sources (White and Murnaghan 1970; Murnaghan and White 1970, 1971). Fear of invasion of privacy has been exacerbated, and has become a politically sensitive issue in some countries where computerized data banks are not only capable of exposing personal health information to quasi-public view, but can also accomplish automatically the compilation of complete records from fragmentary facts, released over a period of time from various sources. The guarded and carefully limited items of medical information, reluctantly provided in the past by physicians, can now be drawn together remotely in precise patterns. They are no longer protected by the file keys of the immediate medical attendant who used to be their only 'owner and guardian' (Lavere 1976).

Even in pragmatic terms the situation requires careful attention and 'unless the medical profession and public can be reassured that no leak or misuse of stored information occurs, or may occur, and that the benefits obtained from health information are required for better functioning of the service, there is a continued likelihood of obstructions' (Alderson 1975). Unfortunately, there are no clear-cut and generally applicable rules of guidance either in pragmatic or in

ethical terms. Nor can there be. A very restrictive policy with respect
to confidentiality can limit even the most rational uses of health
information and deprive future patients of benefits analogous with
those which present patients have derived from information relating
to their predecessors. Even the present patient suffers if health
records relating to different episodes of sickness cannot be assembled
as a guide to his continuous medical care or follow-up. At the other
extreme, a totally utilitarian approach will not only ride roughshod
over sensitive private problems, but will defeat itself through the
opposition and obstruction which it engenders. A compromise
between the two is not therefore to be regarded in any sense as a
'solution', but as an accommodation which is forced upon us by the
fact that no other course of action will suffice. Nor is any general
formulation possible of an appropriate point of balance. The degree
of privacy that can be expected as a 'right' is a function of the total
setting in which an individual finds himself, and is also a function of
the morals of contemporary social systems (Atsumi 1973). The
weight to be placed upon a utilitarian point of view is also dependent
upon the pressures of time and place. Rawls (1973) comments upon
the utilitarian approach in the following terms, 'The principle for an
individual is to advance as far possible his own welfare, his own
system of desires. The principle for society is to advance as far as
possible the welfare of the group, to realize to the greatest extent
the comprehensive system of desire arrived from the desires of its
members. . .Those institutions and acts are right which, of available
alternatives, produce the most good. . .'. The approach expressed
here by Rawls—not necessarily held by him—is deeply at variance
with requirements of individual rights, and the basic issue is that of
balancing the individual's rights or privacy against the rights and needs
of society (Murnaghan and White 1972).

These problems are encountered both in clinical work and in
health care planning and the solutions range from the simple to the
very difficult. A patient with neurosyphilis who refused to be
dissuaded from his occupation of flying jumbo jets would provide
his doctor with a very simple decision, but an applicant for a driving
licence who failed to disclose his well-controlled epilepsy is a more
difficult problem. With health care information systems the problems
are less that doctors are under pressure to disclose highly sensitive
information about a few individuals, but rather to supply data with a
very low individual risk of misuse on a very large scale indeed. In
these situations the main requirements are that information should
not be transmitted for which a legitimate need has not been explicitly
declared, or without the delineation of responsible and accountable

guardianship. There is also a need for explicit operational security standards and this unfortunately, is an area where practice has been lax. Great improvements might often be accomplished simply by assigning special accommodation with limited access and locked doors, or by requiring that records are not held in alphabetic order but in order of an index number, with the alphanumeric key held in a secure place. Rules of access and the definition of authority to release data should also be defined. Computer-supported health information systems are generally far safer than purely manual systems, at least from inadvertent loss or casual theft. They do however lend themselves to the fear (at least) of mass theft or misuse, and even a belief in the possibility is sufficient to impair the functioning of a computerized data system. Although the risks are small they must be taken seriously and must be seen and known to be taken seriously. Indeed, this introduces a problem in that the requirement to publicize the levels of security adopted—which involves some specification of the method—is itself a threat to security. Fortunately, even with demountable magnetic storage devices (e.g. tapes) it is possible to devise encipherment techniques which effectively obscure the meaning of recorded material, and which resist illicit decipherment (Knox 1975; IFIPTC 1975).

10.5. TECHNICAL INNOVATION

Managers and planners of information systems are continually taxed by the conflicting requirements of efficient day-to-day operations and the advancement and development of system design. This dilemma is not of course limited to information systems, but in this area especially the modern technical revolution has exerted particular pressures. With respect to computers, successive generations of technology have followed upon each other at intervals of only a few years, each step offering multiples of previous power for approximately the same cost. As each new data system is 'computerized', and as each old system is re-cycled through maintenance, improvement, and perhaps replacement, probably the greater part of the time and effort of management and senior technical staff has been concerned with development and innovation.

As well as having to cope with the increasing power of successive processors and their increasing rate of obsolescence, data-processing managers have been faced with a widening choice of 'input', 'storage', and 'output' devices. They include punch cards, direct input typewriters, devices for detecting graphite (pencil) marks, magnetic sensing machines, optical sensing machines, 'light pen' inputs to oscilloscope-linked terminals, and so on. The storage devices include magnetic tapes, drums, discs, cards. The output devices include automatic typewriters, line-printers, oscilloscope displays. Some of the automatic outputs can be re-read automatically by the same machine and they find a use in the form of 'return documents'. For example, the output document in a vaccination system may contain a computer printing of the patient's identification and provide a space for indicating completion of the procedure. When it is returned to the computer the machine can read the identification which it originally printed, thus eliminating scope for human error, together with the mark which indicates completion. There are of course many other technical processes concerned with data-processing which have nothing to do with computers at all, chiefly in relation to mechanical file keeping and handling, and a range of addressing devices and magnetic-storage typing (word-processing) machines.

Much of the equipment used for health care information processing was developed for commercial and business applications, and this has to some extent imposed upon health care services, the administrative structures, functions, and philosophies prevalent in these fields. Hierarchically organized business managements, with their main managerial strengths at the centre rather than at the periphery, created a market for large centralized information processors, supplemented in some cases by peripheral units attached by telephone lines. Their adoption in health care management systems for intelligence and control purposes has tended to strengthen a philosophy of centralization in an area where, traditionally, the main professional strengths and volumes of activity have been at the periphery. It is possible, however, that the next round of technical innovation will challenge this movement; the development of mini-computers and micro-computers, providing free-standing systems at greatly reduced costs instead of, as in the past, increasingly powerful systems for similar costs, will create a new situation. If strong central control, and unified intelligence and information systems, are indeed thought to be desirable then they will have to be consciously planned and will not simply follow in the path of an accident of technical history.

10.6. MEETING PLANNING NEEDS

There are many steps between the 'roomfuls of data untouched by human thought', and its assembly into a structured set suitable for the final task of 'extracting good intelligence. . .and getting it into the room where decisions are made' (Wilensky 1967). The transformation process is an extraordinarily complicated exercise which includes the choice of data to be assembled and of the method of acquisition, the choice of suitable techniques for intermediate processing, and its collation, indexing, retrieval, and presentation. These separate procedures interact with each other and serious defects in one part of the chain may vitiate the whole activity. The process as a whole must interact with the health care planning process so that the intelligence system is continually adapted to needs. The interaction is not, however, a one-way process and the exercise will be barren unless planning activities prove to be mutually adaptable.

Experience suggests that these mutual adaptations are difficult to achieve. There is a law of perversity which declares that information needed for a particular purpose is never available and that the information available has no evident use. In practice, the disjunction is seldom so qualitatively exact and the problem can more usually be stated in terms of limited relevance, limited precision, limited specificity, limited reliability, or that the information was not available at the right time, that classifications and groupings were unsuitable, or that data were aggregated in the wrong way, or inappropriately presented. In all such cases, however, the main underlying reason is a lack of coordination between health planners, managers of information systems, and producers of basic data, either through failure to consult, or because of different perceptions of each others' roles. The amelioration of these problems depends upon a continuing (and difficult) mutual education exercise and upon a working relationship in which this can take place.

Dogmatic general statements on the ways of adapting intelligence provision to planning needs, and of obtaining planning responses to the intelligence provided, are seldom very useful. The settings vary too widely. In some countries even the minimum amount of information does not exist, or it does not reach the hands of planners, and such data as are available are unreliable and inaccurate. In the 'developing' countries there is a shortage of competent (e.g. literate) and adequately-trained persons. At primary level the service may employ health auxiliaries with very limited training and education, and often employed for short periods of time. Under these circumstances it is useless for planners to wait for optimal information; they must do their best within their limited resources to identify the purposes to which the information is to be put and to try to adapt it to meet these purposes. Thus, local data of doubtful validity can sometimes be quickly checked through *ad hoc* sampling or by comparison with other countries or regions. Data available from other countries with similar ecological conditions can be adapted or extrapolated (e.g. weight-for-age curves in children). In starting any new major programmes, it is prudent to incorporate facilities for collecting the minimum data required for any further stage of planning and to pay special attention to instructing the appropriate staff and monitoring their performance.

In developed countries the nonconformity between demands for and provisions of intelligence exhibits quite different characteristics. Complex and rapidly changing health care services have an almost limitless requirement for information and well-developed information services have a large capacity for acquisition and processing. The problems which arise are not so much questions of quantity as of quality, timeliness, and relevance. It is here that the discrepancies and dissatisfactions occur. Ways have been proposed for meeting planning requirements without falling into the trap of indulging in yet more data collection. They include regular review of the range of existing data sources and of the frequencies with which they are used. Informed judgements on current and future utility may be obtained through informal enquiry or through explicit procedures such as 'planning games' or the use of the 'Delphi method'. Judgements must also be made concerning the quality of the required data; recent studies have indicated that acceptable project proposals can often be developed on the basis of limited data with less than optimum quality. This is not to minimize the dangers of overmanipulating scanty data or the vulnerability of proposals based upon them to valid objections (WHO 1976).

The acquisition of data is the most costly and labour-intensive item of the process of providing useful information and intelligence. Estimates of the proportion of total hospital budgets spent on this function by professional and clerical workers vary from 25 to 50 per cent. However, the existence of records of transactions does not guarantee eventual transformation to a form useful in decision making. Indeed, information useful to planners, from these sources, is remarkably scarce and either the choice of material, the inter-mediate processes, or the form and pathway of presentation must be at fault. Attempts to control the collection of useless or unused material have given rise to the criterion that information collected should be known to be explicitly needed by those who are responsible for technical planning or administrative decisions. It would follow, then, that the manager of an information system should understand the decision processes of the health programme, and should know what decisions need to be taken, when, and by whom. This is un-exceptionable advice but it is still very often difficult to forecast future uses, not yet envisaged, and even future users. This is impor-tant in an activity with substantial lag times between the assembly and the usage of information. Another difficulty of the 'utility' criterion, in its strictest form, is that it supposes the marriage of planning and of intelligence processing to be a one-way adaptation. This is a dangerous doctrine; the creation of the grounds for a new situational analysis (see § 3.2) through the provision of unsolicited intelligence is a legitimate function of health information management. Investment in health care information systems may be fruitless without a parallel commitment to use the information constructively. Such investment should imply a commitment to improve the effectiveness of the planning and decision-making systems themselves, whether at national, regional, or local community levels (White *et al.* 1977).

Data acquisition, because of its costs, provides the major preoccupation of information-system management. But from the point of view of servicing health care planning the most important tasks concern the assembly, disassembly, reassembly, linkage, and interpretation of existing material. It is vital that the material is presented and interpreted in a manner suitable for the different planning and policy-making bodies (and for the persons(s)) for which it is intended. Sometimes this is achieved by simplification and by aggregating complicated tabular detail, but sometimes it is a question of resurrecting detail which has been lost in an earlier aggregating process. There are many points in a hierarchical organization where the flow of necessary information can be blocked and this may sometimes be done deliberately by lower-level data managers with strong loyalties to their particular units or divisions; alternatively, policy-making levels may be flooded with 'polyaggregated' or unreliable or irrelevant data which confuse and obfuscate. Considerable statistical, data-processing, and epidemiological skills are necessary in order to obtain well-judged numerical presentation, or to decide whether the information should in fact be presented in numerical form, or in a graphical, pictorial, or verbal format. At all levels there is a problem of language. Every discipline tends to develop special languages and special uses of words for the sake of scientific precision, but there is then a tendency to use these technical terms in contexts which do not require them and in which their exact connotations may be misunderstood. The use of 'jargon' impedes real communication in multidisciplinary groups. In groups which include non-professionals, technical language creates feelings of distance, difference, and alienation and actually retards the resolution of common problems. At the same time, technical precision must not be abandoned and presentations of information should try to be educative in these respects.

The processes of aggregation and generalization required at successively superior levels of a complex planning organization, are usually accompanied by shifts of interest from functionally-defined towards institutionally-defined formulations (§ 4.2), from shorter-term to longer-term projections, from budgetary to economic, and from technical to political considerations, and from local to general constraints upon growth, and upon freedom of action. It is therefore a mistake to suppose that the progressive adaptation of data from these different purposes is simply a question of aggregation. On the contrary, new and different sources, and especially external sources, need to be tapped at each level. It is as mistaken for an intelligence system, as it is for the health care planning system itself, to suppose that it is structured along the lines of a single hierarchy. The matrix structure outlined in §4.2 is as valid for one, as for the other.

As we saw above, the reconstruction of numerical information for different planning levels involves a blend of statistical procedures—the aggregation of tables, numerical addition, simplification of taxonomy, deletion of detail, and, to some extent, the introduction of new material. However, utility and reliability at all levels depend upon the ways in which the basic data were observed, classified, and coded. Sound presentations of material for planning purposes should in general provide some assessment of the reliability with which these primary functions were carried out. In the long run there is nothing more damaging to the functions of an intelligence system than presentations containing errors of fact or of interpretation which the users can see for themselves but which those responsible for presentation fail to see or to point out. At the lowest level an appraisal of reliability might include an account of the manner in which the data were collected and classified, noting for example that the diagnostic classifications were carried out by untrained clerical staff rather than by physicians in charge. At the processing level it could be noted that absence of a unique identifier prevented information on consultations being converted into information on patients, or that the absence of a unique numbering system covering a group of hospitals precluded checks upon the extent to which patients encountered in one hospital were the same people as those encountered in another. At the level of interpretation there are many difficulties in adapting information to purposes for which it was not primarily intended. A common error arises from attempts to use hospital in-patient statistics as measures of morbidity in the population living in the area surrounding the hospital; this is inaccurate and may be misleading. It may be possible to overcome these and similar difficulties, but if not, then a first duty is to say that they exist (or at best have not been excluded) and what the consequences are.

Planning teams have a right to be presented with reservations and circumspections such as these, together with an overall assessment of the reliance which can be placed upon any given set of data. Those who manage the information systems are often the only ones who are in a position to provide it, and the planners have to rely upon the judgements of their information teams in these matters. In particular, the processes of drawing inferences and conclusions from population data are subject to risks of error in many subtle and important ways and both skill and experience are necessary if the traps are to be avoided. The necessary professional skills are associated largely, if not entirely, with the discipline of epidemiology. This forms the subject matter of the next part of this book.

PART III

The scope and applications of epidemiology

11. The methods of epidemiology

11.1. INTRODUCTION

It is our purpose in this part to display the concepts, scope, and methods of the discipline of epidemiology. We hope to help politicians, clinicians, administrators, and other professional groups, to recognize the contributions to planning which they might reasonably expect from its practitioners. To this end we shall concentrate upon examples and activities related to health care planning and we also hope to demonstrate to epidemiologists who have not engaged in this field, what modifications of approach and technique they will need to develop if they wish to participate.

Epidemiology has been defined as 'the study of the distribution of disease and disability in human populations and of the factors which influence that distribution' (Hogarth 1975). We pointed out in the Introduction, however, that the discipline has evolved rather rapidly over the last few decades, and concise definitions of this kind have only a limited value. This part is designed to expand the definition of the subject and is organized to attain three objectives. First, it describes the fundamental reasoning of the discipline, and the nature of its scientific and technical foundations. Second, it describes the main types of problem in which epidemiologists concerned with health care tend to engage. Third, it analyses and comments upon the limitations of epidemiology, indicating both the technical constraints and the conceptual limits.

We hope through this presentation, and through the accounts of planning and of information services provided in Parts I and II, to lay the foundations for a discussion of the working relationships between epidemiologists, health statisticians, managers, and other specialists concerned in planning. This discussion will be developed in Part IV. However, there is one implicit assumption which should be evident at this stage and is best stated now. That is, we do not see the delineation of the epidemiological contribution in terms of a sectorial division of the planning cycle. The epidemiologist is concerned not solely with the monitoring and evaluation of existing services—although these are of special interest—but with the planning process in its entirety, including the assessment of needs, the formulation of and choice between alternative policies and objectives, with evaluation, with the design of experimental services, and with the implementation and development of definitive ones. However, the declaration and acceptance of this global responsibility is not in any sense a claim for exclusivity. The contributions of epidemiology intersect with those of other disciplines. Thus, many points of detail in the following discussion will be recognized as basically scientific rather than specifically epidemiological.

11.2. THE BASIC REASONING OF EPIDEMIOLOGY

The distinctive characteristic of epidemiology is a concern with health and sickness in populations and groups. This concern is based upon the premise that these phenomena exhibit certain features and certain types of behaviour which can be expressed only in population terms, and whose study may lead to means of control or to more effective care. W.H. Frost (1927) expressed this fact many years ago when he said that 'there is for each disease a set of epidemiological characteristics just as distinctive as its clinical characteristics and serving equally well, if the description were adequate, to differentiate it from other diseases'.

The standard measures of sickness in populations—prevalences and attack rates—are essentially statistical. Population expressions of quantitative attributes such as height, weight, I.Q., or blood pressure, are also expressed in statistical terms through the use of means (averages) and distributions (centiles, standard deviations, histograms, etc.). Where more than one attribute is recorded in one person (for example, (a) the occurrence or non-occurrence of a stroke, and (b) the preceding level of blood pressure) the population approach gives rise to the quantitative concept of association. That is, the risk of stroke is shown to differ for different levels of blood pressure. The concept of association is one from which inferences about the causes of certain diseases may sometimes be drawn.

Places and times of events such as disease onsets, or requests for medical advice, also give rise to large-scale phenomena. These phenomena find expression in terms of demonstrated geographical distributions, time plots, upward and downward trends, seasonal cycles, irregular time clusters, contact patterns and connections between events, proximity patterns in relation to sources of hazard (e.g. disease occurrences surrounding a source of a dangerous pollutant), and all the other complex time/space phenomena which constitute the concept of epidemicity. We are not limited in the use of the concept to the infectious diseases, but may apply it also to 'outbreaks' of acute poisoning, as at Seveso (Hay, 1976a, b, c), of behavioural disorders such as heroin addiction (Reynolds *et al.* 1976; Roy. Soc. Med, and Roy. Soc. Med Inc. 1973), of iatrogenic diseases such as thalidomide malformations (Lenz 1961; McBride 1961; Lenz and Knapp 1962), and others.

Errors of medical observations—an important subject for epidemiological study—are also expressed in terms which transcend approaches appropriate to individual patients. The question is not so much *whether* a mistake has been made, but rather *how often* this occurs. The notion of *repeatability* of observations is essential, including the question of the extent to which one observer's records match those of another, the extent to which an observer can match his own previous assessment on a second occasion, and the degree to which a new and simpler form of examination (for example) can match the results of a more elaborate and expensive one. For some observations the epidemiologist will be concerned with more than one kind of error. In a breast cancer detection programme, for example, he is concerned not only with the proportion of true cases missed, but with the proportion of normal women who receive an unnecessary biopsy.

The *models* used by epidemiologists are also set in large-number terms. A characteristic approach is to use observations and measurements carried out on samples, as representing (i.e. modelling) the population from which the sample was drawn. Statistical procedures for estimating the reliability of samples for this purpose are central to the epidemiologist's technical repertoire. Causal models are also widely used, as they are in other areas of medicine and in other sciences, but again, characteristically, they are set in 'large-number' terms. The essential concept here is that of 'risk', expressed in quantitative/probabilistic terms. Models of this general type are used both by epidemiologists concerned with the biological problems of the causation of disease (with an eye to their prevention), and by those concerned mainly with assessing needs for medical care (with an eye to providing or deploying resources to meet these needs). For both kinds of work extremely complex models, which defy the delineation of exact causes, may sometimes be necessary. Epidemiology has sometimes been described as medical ecology, involving a system of which the basic components are physical, social, and biological. Whenever a new element enters or leaves an ecosystem the balance of all the remaining constituents is disturbed and a new and different reaction results. It is often impossible, on the basis of a single investigation, to measure precisely the influence of one component upon another, and epidemiologists frequently use a battery of different data sets and a battery of analytical techniques in order to dissect the situation. They also use models for purposes of extrapolation, in order to transfer conclusions from one location to another, from one social context to another, and from one time to another. This last group of applications includes the science and art of prediction, an activity especially relevant to the context of planning.

In the light of the conceptual framework outlined above it is easy to understand why epidemiologists also see one of the appropriate outlets for their scientific endeavours to be in population terms, that is, in the provision of services. Those with special interests in developing valid causal models of disease processes have seen their chief outlets in preventive services. Those who have tried to develop an understanding of the interactions between sick people and the health care services have naturally seen the outlets in this second area. In both cases, however, the objective is to produce large-scale effects through complex social, environmental, or medical care systems, the effects being also expressed in 'mass' terms: reduced prevalence, reduced attack rate, improved health status, increased effectiveness, improved accessibility, better standards of care.

The practical applications which spring from these concepts and approaches demand from epidemiologists a substantial body of scientific and technical skills, and we shall describe them below. It is not our purpose to lay them out as a practical manual; this is outside our objectives and, in any case, texts are available elsewhere. Our chief purpose is to enable readers who are not already familiar with the field to appreciate the kinds of skills which epidemiologists may bring to the planning and development of health care services, and to indicate to epidemiologists who have not yet entered this field, the ways in which they may modify their technical repertoires.

11.3. MEASUREMENT OF SICKNESS AND OF MEDICAL NEED

The technical aspects of making observations, recording and collecting data, processing the data, and measuring frequencies in populations are identical in each of the fields with which epidemiologists are concerned. Thus, an epidemiologist familiar with either the biological or the health care field will have no difficulty in using his existing skills in the other.

Epidemiological observations are based upon two distinct classes of phenomena which we may refer to as 'states' and 'events'. A 'state' is defined in terms of a single attribute or a set of attributes and requires the allocation of a patient or a potential client to a particular class within an existing taxonomy. Thus, the basic observation is an act of 'recognition'. Examples are 'has diabetes', 'is severely disabled', 'is at risk of cerebral hemorrhage', 'is in need of advice', or 'is on the waiting list'. The problem of deriving the taxonomy (i.e. the classification system) may be quite simple; sometimes, however, it is a subtle and demanding task, and we shall return to this presently.

'Events' are more complex than 'states' and they are observed in one of two ways. First they may be observed directly and the record might take the form 'hit by car', 'died of tuberculosis', or 'brought in by ambulance'. The second way of observing an event is an indirect one and consists in noting a 'change of state' between two occasions. Examples are 'has developed a varicose ulcer', 'has recovered', or 'has become more urgent'.

There are various permutations of the modes of observation of states and events, and more complex constructs like 'episodes' or 'spells' involve at least two changes of state, from normal to sick and back again, and some illnesses like asthma or epilepsy are actually defined in episodic terms. A 'syndrome', although a complex construct, is (usually) static and is in fact a complex state.

A 'disease' is a much more complex idea than any of these. It carries a connotation of process, whether this be a natural history expressible only in clinical terms—as in mental illness—or whether it be expressible also in terms of a macroscopic or microscopic spectrum, or sequence, of tissue changes. In addition, it demands characterization in terms outside its clinical description—that is, it requires some external point of reference to distinguish it, simply, from a syndrome. If this is not in pathological, parasitic, or microbiological terms, then it must be in terms of its epidemiological or genetic characteristics.

The importance of these distinctions is that population frequency measurements for each of these constructs require their own distinctive approaches, and, if the correct approach is not used, the answer is either erroneous or unobtainable. In practice mistakes are frequently made and wrong conclusions frequently drawn.

Briefly, a state can be recognized at a point in time and does not require a prolonged period of observation. By contrast, the recognition of an event requires either a continuous period of observation so that the event can be observed directly, or else a succession of observations so that changes can be inferred. In the latter case the timing of the event will be uncertain to some degree, the resolution depending upon the frequency with which the observations were repeated. The frequency of a state in a population can be expressed as a simple proportion, usually referred to as a 'prevalence' or a 'point prevalence'. For example, 'the prevalence of umbilical hernia in a sample of 6-month-old children was 60 per thousand'. For events, which are detected on the basis of observations spread over a period of time, the measure of frequency must also, itself, include time.

For example, 'the out-patient attendance rate of a sample of children under five years old was 75 per thousand per annum'.

The intricacies of assembling a set of time-dimensioned (i.e. rates) and non-time-dimensioned (i.e. prevalence) estimates of frequencies of disease, demand, needs, and resources, in order to provide a basis for rational planning, is often a complex task. The skills, understanding, and techniques which an experienced epidemiologist can bring are indispensable for this purpose.

11.4. TAXONOMY AND CLASSIFICATION

The primary operations for measuring the frequency of disease, demand, or need, are recognition, recording, and counting. Recognition is the process of observing and allocating the observation to a 'class', and the process of classification depends upon the existence of a defined set of classes, that is a taxonomy. The processes of devising a taxonomy and of classifying observations are fundamental scientific activities, not least in epidemiology and in health care studies.

The simplest taxonomies are binary (sick or well: dead or alive), or extended uni-dimensional schemes (recovered, improved, same, worse, dead). Implied orderings are present in some (e.g. socio-economic groups), but not in others. Some are based upon qualitative and some upon quantitative criteria (e.g. birth-weight groups).

In some circumstances individuals are classified simultaneously on two scales (e.g. an age scale and a scale of frequency of demands made upon services) and this lends itself to the construction of two-dimensional matrices. Some investigations require the construction of multi-dimensional matrices. However, many biological and social taxonomies do not lend themselves easily to simple matrices in which all the classes of one taxonomy interact with all the classes of another in a simple chess board (orthogonal) pattern. Often, each of the classes of the first taxonomy will require a different *system* of classification at the next stage. Such is the case with medical diagnostic systems. For example, having divided patients into 'mentally ill' and 'physically ill', each division is found to require a different system of sub-classification.

Most taxonomies are constructed on intuitive grounds, for particular purposes, although in recent years there has been a development of computer methods (i.e. numerical taxonomy techniques). Some taxonomies, developed and validated over periods of years have become 'standard'. They include the International Classification of Diseases (ICD), the Standardized Nomenclature of Pathology (SNOP), and the Registrar General of England and Wales' social classification according to occupation.

Two technical points may be made on the usage of taxonomic systems. First, there is no such thing as a 'correct' taxonomy in any field whatsoever; a taxonomy is judged on its utility, and its utility must be judged in relation to a defined objective. Second, taxonomies need to be validated; that is, it is necessary to enquire whether the definitions of the classes are sufficiently exact to permit consistency of classification. This is usually tested by carrying out the operation more than once, either in the hands of different observers or, with suitable safeguards, by the same observer on separate occasions. Studies of these kinds have given rise to a large and important scientific literature under the general titles of 'observer variation' and 'observer error'. It should go without saying, although it more often goes without recognition, that unless an observation is repeatable it cannot be said to be measuring anything at all.

Sufficient has been said to indicate that this is a complex technical field with considerable scope for error. This is true both in biological and health care studies. Fortunately, the principles and techniques for handling these problems are the same in both areas and, from the point of view of an epidemiologist, transfer of interest from one area to the other should create few problems. The main differences are in subject matter rather than in technique; there is a special concern, in health care studies, with the classification of needs, types of demand, levels of disability, tasks, and activities, rather than with disease diagnosis and the classification of putative causal factors.

11.5. POPULATIONS AND SAMPLES

It is implicit in the epidemiological approach to health and health care problems that both the questions and the answers must be related to defined populations. Sometimes the populations have simply to be identified and carefully counted. How many people with artificial limbs are there in the community? How many people present in a year with inguinal hernia? How many admissions occur in a month from ischaemic heart disease? On other occasions, both a sick population and a total population have to be identified, and the one related to the other. What *proportion* of the population attends for medical care in a year? What is the *rate* of occurrence, per thousand working population, of industrial accidents requiring transfer to hospital?

It is frequently necessary to characterize the members of a previously defined population according to some more or less complex criterion. What is the extension of life achieved in patients with cardiac pace-makers? What is the effect upon requirements for educational resources of routinely applied neonatal surgery in infants with spina bifida? What is the balance of benefit and harm in women undergoing mammographic screening for breast cancer? In such cases the population to be studied is defined by the question asked. But identification and enumeration, as opposed to definition, are more difficult matters. National census material, birth and death registrations, hospital admissions and diagnostic indexes, and item-of-service records may be suitable aids when they exist. Electoral registers, insurance schemes, employment registers, and house-holders address registries also supply bases, although selective, from which certain populations may be identified. In countries where documentary materials of these kinds do not exist, and where even personal identification is inexact, *ad hoc* identification via door-to-door contact may have to be undertaken.

Care, as well as ingenuity, are required in such investigations. For example, study of a general practice population will give entirely different results in circumstances where every patient registers in order to obtain care 'free at the point of demand', and in circumstances where registration is deferred until the first demand is made. Problems also arise when populations are selected at a point of time (for example an employment registry), but where the characterization of the population is to be in terms of observations requiring a period of time. The relationship between treatment, costs, and outcomes for mental disorders requiring admission to hospital will look entirely different depending upon whether the study population is defined in terms of admissions, of discharges, or of current occupancy of a bed. The measurement of the latent interval between exposure to an industrial hazard and its resulting disease will also look different in an investigation which begins with the hazard and investigates the consequence, than in an investigation which begins with the effect and searches for the antecedent hazard.

For many investigations it is not necessary to examine the total population, but rather a sample. It is usually necessary to ensure that this sample is selected in an unbiased manner and as a defined pro-portion of the universe to which the results of its investigation will subsequently be applied. Sometimes, different sections of the popu-lation (age groups, geographical areas) are sampled at different frequencies, and sometimes different times, and there is a body of well-developed technique for designing samples in order to improve the efficiency of such investigations. These techniques are not of course the special province of epidemiology, and are used by many other population scientists. However, one method of special interest to epidemiologists is the use of related samples taken for comparative purposes. For every case defined in a particular way, an attempt is made to select one or more similar people, differing in respect of the attribute of interest, but similar in as many other respects as possible.

For example, an investigation was carried out to see whether there was an occupational predisposition to herniated lumbar intervertebral disc (Kelsey 1975). A sample was taken of hospital patients who had lumbar X-rays and who were thought to have this condition. Two 'comparison samples' were also taken, one consisting of 'next' admissions of persons in the same sex and age group, and the second consisting of those who had an X-ray but were not thought to have a herniated disc. Investigations such as these are recognized as 'untidy' in that the investigator can never be certain to what extent the groups differ on criteria other than those of prime interest (the herniated disc). He is never certain how far an apparent association between a putative 'cause and an effect can be trusted, and usually has to spend a great deal of time investigating other possible explanations. Pragmatically, however, it is an economic and powerful technique, and with the justification of its successes behind it, it continues to be widely used.

11.6. EPIDEMIOLOGICAL INFERENCE

Inference is the process of arguing from the particular to the general. It requires the formulation of hypotheses in explanation of facts observed. A hypothesis can be used in the deductive process of predicting consequences in other situations. The hypothesis can then be tested by seeing whether the predictions are matched by facts. Provided that the hypothesis is accurately stated, the deductive process follows formal rules and is in this sense logical. By contrast, the process of inference is without formal rules of procedure, and in this sense in extra-logical. These processes are totally general and apply in all branches of science.

The process of arguing from samples to populations is a form of inference described, usually, as 'statistical inference', although it is based in fact upon a *deductive* process. It is possible to calculate the effects of defined sampling procedures upon a population whose structure is known, and to express the outcome as a range of alternatives, each with a different probability. The larger the sample, the closer will be its structure, on average, to that of the parent population. Statistical inference depends upon reversing this argument so that, given a knowledge of a sample, the probable range of findings in the parent population can then be stated. It is a form of reasoning which has resulted in a large development of statistical arithmetic, centred on the notions of 'statistical significance' and of 'confidence limits'.

In fact, reversal of the population-to-sample argument is logically unsound, and statistical inference, like other forms of inference, remains an extra-logical procedure. Unfortunately, this has not been recognized as widely as it might have been and there has been a great deal of misunderstanding and misstatement of the issues involved. The problem can best be illustrated by an example.

Where a sample of matched pairs is drawn from a general population (as in the lumbar disc problem given above) and where the prevalence of some attribute differs between the 'cases' and 'controls', we would like guidance as to whether the difference could be a consequence of the sampling procedures alone. The standard practice is to set up the so called 'null hypothesis'—the hypothesis that there are no systematic differences in the population from which the sample was drawn. We can then calculate, using standard tests, the probability of a sample exhibiting the observed difference, if that hypothesis were true. If the probability is very small we have intuitive cause to doubt the null hypothesis, and therefore to suppose that there is in fact a difference in the parent population. Two things, however, should be clearly understood. First, the calculated probability is not directly applicable to the parent population or to any hypothesis other than the null hypothesis, and it does not constitute a statement of the probability of the null hypothesis being right or wrong. Second, statistical inference is purely descriptive; it is an attempt to specify the characteristics of a population on the basis of observations made in a sample and it has nothing to do with causes or mechanisms, even where statistical associations have been demonstrated.

The issues of causal inference are entirely unrelated to statistical inference. The only point of similarity is that this too is an intuitive process. It is almost always based upon a battery of investigative approaches rather than upon a single one, and upon a body of external knowledge derived from clinical, chemical, pathological, microbiological, behavioural, and other sources. The battery of epidemiological investigations will usually include enquiry as to 'time, place, and person.' That is, the investigator will establish *where* a disease occurs, whether it shows geographical gradients, or whether it is concentrated in the vicinity of particular geographical features. He will discover *when* it occurs, whether it shows long-term increases or decreases of frequency, whether it shows seasonal, weekly, or diurnal cycles, or whether it shows irregular clusters. He will also ascertain in *what sort of person* it occurs, how it varies with age and sex, whether it is associated with personal characteristics such as height or intelligence, or with social characteristics such as occupation, or with the physical characteristics of the person's environment, including his housing, and records of exposure to occupational hazards. Studies will be carried out upon interactions between time, place, and person. That is, the investigator will wish to know whether a time trend (for instance) is occurring at all ages, or just at some; he will wish to know whether geographical clusters occur repeatedly in the same place or whether they are in different places at different times. He will also wish to see some investigations repeated and to see some findings confirmed from different points of view. For all these kinds of investigation there is a large body of established technique and a large scientific literature recording successful and unsuccessful attempts at their application, and both accurate and inaccurate interpretations of results.

An epidemiologist in the field of health care planning is probably less concerned with causal inference than one whose chief concern is with preventive work. In preventive work the discovery of causes is central. For health care research and planning a great deal may be obtained from simple descriptive studies. Where causal mechanisms are postulated they are very often sociological and behavioural in character rather than concerned with the aetiologies of the diseases themselves. One major exception is in the investigation of the ill effects of medical care, the so called 'iatrogenic' diseases.

11.7. NON-EXPERIMENTAL APPROACHES TO PROBLEMS

The majority of epidemiological investigations, whether into biological or into health care topics, are 'observational' and 'descriptive'. That is, relatively few are manipulative (i.e. experimental), and fewer still consist of extrapolations and projections based upon formal models (we deal with these two processes later).

Many scientific questions demand only a numerical or a graphical description based upon simple data collection, simple classification, and counting. The outcomes consist of measures of disease frequencies, statements of geographical distributions, measures of rates of demand upon services, distances travelled, time spent, costs incurred, numbers on waiting lists, times spent on waiting lists, percentage bed-occupancies in different specialities, distributions of bed-occupancy times for different diagnoses, and so on. The sources and uses of such material were set out in Part II.

However, not all descriptive tasks are simple and some require quite intricate interpretations. For example, an attack rate or a demand rate which changes with age may not be all that it seems. The onset of carcinoma-in-situ of the cervix has been observed in many communities to rise in successive age groups up to about age

35, and to fall progressively thereafter. How do we interpret this finding? Does it represent a rise and fall in risk in individual women passing from age 20 to age 50? Or does it represent a changing pattern of experience such that today's younger women are quite different from today's older women: the older women have low attack rates not so much because they have passed through a period of higher risk, but because they had a relatively low risk throughout. In other words we have to distinguish a (so-called) cohort effect from a natural-history sequence. Graphical techniques have been developed (given sufficient data) for distinguishing between these possibilities, and they have been applied with conspicuous success in the study of tuberculosis, lung cancer, growth and development characteristics, cervical cancer risks, Parkinson's disease, and others. They illuminate both the natural history of these diseases, and the effects of changing social conditions and improving medical services. They provide a basis for displaying the relative importance of these effects and provide a rationale for projecting future medical needs.

The separation of interacting relationships, of which the cohort effect is one example, is a general problem in epidemiological studies and is encountered in many situations. Thus, the incidence of a disease is found to vary in different geographical locations. The age distribution also varies in geographical locations. Finally, the incidence varies according to age. The task consists in discovering whether the varied incidence in different geographical locations is entirely secondary to the differing age distributions, or whether there is some more fundamental variation in risk. Problems such as this are handled through a range of manoeuvres known collectively as 'standardization' procedures.

In a geographical problem of this kind it is necessary to define a 'reference' or 'standard' population, possibly the national population, with which the populations of individual areas could be compared. An 'indirect' standardization method would be used; the attack rates within each age/sex group of the standard population are multiplied by the numbers in each age/sex group of the local populations to calculate how many cases would have occurred if the national rate had applied. The local numbers actually observed, divided by the expected values, provide an index of relative morbidity from which the effects of the local age/sex distribution have been removed. (In the case of deaths, these ratios are usually multiplied by 100 and presented as 'standardized mortality ratios'.)

Although the standardized mortality ratio (SMR) is the best-known example of an indirect standardization technique, such methods are used in a wide variety of other circumstances. Standardization can be carried out according to occupation, socio-economic group, ethnic origin, and a wide range of other factors. If, for example, a series of maternity units displays variation in the perinatal mortality rate, part of the explanation could lie in the fact that different units have different types of clientele such that the birth-weight distributions of the infants vary between them. The proportions of multiple births could also vary, and so could the birth rank distributions and maternal age distributions. Each of these factors is known to affect perinatal mortality expectations. It is possible through indirect standardization to calculate standardized indices of performance which allow for one or more of the relevant factors. It may be found that an apparently poor performance is adequately explained in terms external to the care received in the unit; conversely, it may be found that in some units a poor performance has been masked by favourable external conditions.

Standarization procedures are usually used as part of an attempt to draw causal inferences. The validity of their use therefore depends upon the validity with which a causal model can be envisaged. In some studies of complex interactions between different factors the investigators will quite properly resist the temptation to draw conclusions about causes, will avoid the use of standardization techniques, and will content themselves with a simple display. For example, in the complex area of childhood development a very large series of interactions may be demonstrated between maternal age, paternal age, birth rank, birth weight, weight and height on successive birthdays, age of menarche in females, intelligence quotients at successive ages, parental intelligence, parental heights and weights, sickness experience in the first five years, and so on. Situations of similar complexity may also be observed in the development of patterns of demand for medical care. Formal statistical methods offer no automatic solutions and prudent investigators will avoid the trap of drawing exact cause and effect conclusions.

A characteristic approach to the testing of well-defined causal hypotheses (as in the 'lumbar-disc' example) is to select sets of 'cases' and 'controls' for comparison. There are two basic kinds of field technique, and they are usually described as prospective and retrospective. In a retrospective study patients may be selected because of a particular disease (e.g. lung cancer). One, or probably several, sets of 'controls' without lung cancer are then chosen in such a way that they are as like to the patients as is possible in respect of all other characteristics. Enquiry is then made of both groups of the presence or absence of suspected antecedent causes, such as tobacco smoking, radiation exposure, occupational oil-mist exposure, and so on. In health care research the usual starting point for a case/control study will be the delivery of an item of service, such as blood transfusion or an anxiolytic drug; there will be a double interest which covers both the question why the disease occurred, and why the patient presented at a particular place at a particular time in a particular way.

Retrospective studies have the advantage that if they are possible at all, they are relatively quick to perform. Indeed the necessary data may already have been recorded. They have the disadvantage that if the required data have not been recorded, they may by now be impossible to get; the patients or their relatives may be dead. Patient 'survival' problems also affect retrospective studies. If the initial population is acquired through a cross-sectional type of survey —for example through measuring blood pressure or estimating serum cholesterol—the sub-group with high values may already have been decimated, and the survivors be quite unrepresentative. Their comparison with 'normals' will give deceptive results. If electro-cardiograms are performed on railway workers it may be found that ticket collectors have a higher rate of ischaemic changes than do plate-layers. Can it then be concluded that the physical exercise of plate laying is protective? An alternative hypothesis is that plate-layers with ischaemic changes are more likely to have left the industry because of inability to continue in heavy labour, than have ticket collectors with the same disease. Indeed, the breathless plate-layers may have become ticket collectors!

In prospective studies the investigator begins with a set of people who are exposed to a postulated risk, and with matched sets of controls not so exposed. Well-designed prospective studies usually succeed in overcoming the 'survival' problem. However, they have other disadvantages. First they often take years to complete and, especially in health care planning, a conclusion may not be available until after the point of necessary decision. Prospective studies also tend to be expensive. They share with retrospective ones the problem that groups which are known to be different with respect to a feature of interest (e.g. blood pressure) are also certainly different in other, and possibly unknown, respects. This is still true even when a matched-pairs type of study is undertaken. Prospective investigations in the field of health care have a special problem of their own. This arises from the highly interactive circumstances in which they are carried out. For example, the introduction of a cervical cytology screening programme usually depends upon a highly developed gynaecological service with higher standards of clinical diagnosis, of accessibility, and of treatment, than elsewhere. It will also be accompanied by a high hysterectomy rate for reasons other than cervical cancer. Each of these additional factors, as well as the cytology service itself, is capable of reducing mortality from cervical cancer, and a comparison between areas with and without a cytology screening service cannot readily conclude that differential improvements in mortality are due to the service itself. A number of subsidiary analyses will be necessary, and an investigator might hope to use experimental and retrospective studies as well as the prospective approach. There are many examples like this. The question of the utility of tonsillectomy and adenoidectomy in the majority of children on whom it is practised, has remained a largely intractable question for reasons such as these.

Not all case control studies fall neatly into the retrospective/prospective dichotomy. Sometimes, a large amount of data may already exist concerning previous levels of exposure to a risk. Environmental exposures to lead in different parts of a city may have been recorded and may be linkable with place-of-birth data, and with subsequently collected data on school performance. Groups of children suffering extremes of early lead exposure are subsequently identified and their mean 'subsequent I.Q.'-levels calculated. Although the data exist in retrospect it is clear that the formal plan of the analysis is prospective.

Analytical studies of cause and effect are not limited to materials which demonstrate associations between variables within the same individual. Studies of spatio–temporal connectivities between events provide additional scope for the analytical approach. They are especially relevant where diseases are known to be infective, or toxic, or where it is suspected that they might be. Population genetic analysis—another dimension for studying connectivities between people and between events—provides yet another basis for this kind of study, although one which is possibly not so relevant to health care planning as some of those already outlined.

11.8. DESIGN AND MANAGEMENT OF EXPERIMENTS

An experiment is defined as an investigation based upon a manipulation. Its purpose is to discover the effect of the manipulation. Since health care planning leads to manipulations of the way in which the service operates, and because the evaluation of outcomes is an essential part of the planning cycle, the possibilities of carrying out experiments have a very direct appeal.

There is an intellectual and philosophical attraction, too. The notion of a cause, although central to inductive thinking, is an elusive one. There are no logical tests for determining when and whether a sequence of events is causally related, except for the observation that the supposed cause consistently precedes the supposed effect. Even the requirement of consistency is 'soft' in that, while the order must always be the same, the association does not have to be universal. Thus, we speak of a 'necessary' cause when the cause must *always* be present if the event is to occur, but not all causes are necessary. There may be alternative causes. We speak of cause as 'sufficient' when, if it occurs, the effect will always follow, but not all causes are sufficient. They may only operate in the presence of appropriate external circumstances. In most etiological studies of disease, and in most studies of the determinants of health care demand and usage, the inferred 'causes' are neither sufficient nor necessary and are observed as probabilistic sequential associations. Causal hypotheses in these fields are therefore often judged more on the criterion of 'utility' rather than the criterion of 'truth', and experimentation provides the pathway to this judgement. The very notion of a 'cause' is closely linked with the possibility of manipulating the circumstances in which it is supposed to operate.

One particular class of experimental design has won a central place in human studies and this is the 'randomized controlled trial' (RCT). Its main premise, as applied to clinical studies of the efficacy of drugs, is that while no two individuals may be sufficiently alike to compare the effect of giving the drug to one with the effect of not giving it to the other, it should be possible to assemble *groups* of treated and untreated patients which are sufficiently alike in all respects other than the treatment, to permit such comparisons to be made. The similarity of the groups is achieved through a 'randomization' process whereby patients are allocated to the 'treated' or the 'untreated' group according to some random process—e.g. alternately on admission, or according to odd or even dates of birth, or according to the oddness or evenness of the next number from a table of random numbers. Where possible, the choice of treatment is hidden from the patient. Where possible it is hidden also from the person responsible for assessing the outcome. Where these two bias-avoiding procedures can be incorporated into the design the trial is known as a 'double blind' RCT.

The attraction of the approach is that, where a difference in outcome is detected between 'cases' and 'controls', it can be due to only one of two causes, either the effect of the drug or the inaccuracies of the randomization process. There are statistical tests for dealing with the likelihood that the latter alone could produce a particular result and, since there are only two alternatives, interpretation is relatively uncomplicated. This is in contrast to the observations which might be made in a prospective but non-experimental study.

Here, in addition to the possible effect of random processes in the sampling procedures, there are many other known and unknown differences between the groups.

The RCT is not a perfect instrument, particularly in health care planning. It has an important place, but a limited one. First, like all prospective studies, it tends to be time-consuming, and may not provide answers until after the point of decision has been reached. Second, especially when applied to testing the effectiveness of services, as opposed to the efficacy of procedures, successful implementation requires a degree of control which may be unrealistic. Third, experiments carried out on a service scale (e.g. the effectiveness of a service for the early diagnosis and treatment of hypertension) usually require a level of background knowledge in justification of the experiment, which is almost sufficient to justify a definitive service. The level of knowledge required to justify providing the service to half the people, makes it difficult to justify withholding it from the other half.

Fourth, the question of effectiveness often arises with respect to services which are already being supplied (e.g. radiotherapy for certain tumours, adeno-tonsillectomy, orchidopexy, routine school health examinations, etc.) and it may be difficult to obtain a sufficient consensus on their probable *lack* of utility, to mount a formal experiment. Finally, it may be technically inefficient, even when an experiment is possible, to apply it to testing the effectiveness of a service as a whole. It may be better to apply the experimental approach to its components, and to assemble a judgement on the total service upon the basis of the theoretical background which has thereby been strengthened. For example, one measure of the effectiveness of an automated biochemistry service might be seen as shortened durations of stay in hospital. A direct trial, different hospital units being randomly allocated or not allocated to a routine investigation regime, then shows no difference. On second thoughts it is found that there were other critical constraints determining the date of discharge, possibly the visiting rotas of physicians-in-charge. Thus, while it would be perfectly true to say that under the particular conditions the system of biochemical investigation made no difference with respect to discharge, it might under somewhat different circumstances have done so. It might therefore have been better to base the investigation upon some other component or index of outcome, for example the date on which the final diagnosis was recorded.

Despite the difficulties, RCT's have been applied successfully to a number of important health care problems. The Health Insurance Plan (HIP) studies of breast cancer screening in New York (Shapiro *et al.* 1973) demonstrated the effectiveness of early diagnosis in achieving a reduced mortality. Trials of lung cancer screening using mass miniature radiography (MMR) in London (Brett 1968) demonstrated that while a higher rate of surgical resectability was obtained, there was no effect upon mortality. For service planning purposes both investigations left a range of pertinent questions unanswered, but the situation was infinitely clearer than was the case with respect to cervical cytology screening, where no randomized trial of effectiveness has ever been reported.

Not all experiments are of the randomized controlled type, although the uncertainties of interpretation of almost all other kinds, and especially of 'before and after' experiments, has led some authors to use the term 'quasi-experiment' in these contexts. Nevertheless, with due care, they can be extremely useful (Campbell and Stanley 1963).

There are several examples of investigations of fatal motor accidents in which data were collected before and after the compulsory fitting of seat belts to motor vehicles, or legislation requiring them to be worn. A sharp departure of the 'after' from 'before' trend provides evidence that the legislation accomplished its purpose, if no other causes of the departure can be identified. Such evidence is greatly strengthened if similar breaks in time trends are observed in different countries or regions which introduce legislation in different years. Similar studies and arguments have been applied to legislation on blood alcohol limits in drivers and to the effectiveness of diphtheria toxoid in preventing diphtheria. Crucial to such 'quasi-experiments' is the collection of objective data which are safe from distortion by those who might wish to reach a prejudged conclusion.

The above examples relate to 'health and prevention' more specifically than to health care, and examples in the latter field have been more often proposed than successfully executed. Where they have been carried out they have often been suceptible to alternative interpretations as in the examples of cervical cytology screening, automated laboratories, hospital computers, and others.

In many prospective studies, both experimental and non-experimental, the investigator alters the circumstances of the study simply by his presence. Depending upon the objectives, it may be necessary to minimize this effect; the randomized controlled trial is one way of doing this. In other circumstances, especially where a programme of alternating investigations and implementations is envisaged, the argument for trying to do so is less tenable. Sometimes, the research is consciously used as the agent of change. The term 'action research' has come to be applied to developments of these kinds. An example might be a series of experiments into ways in which institutionalized mentally subnormal children can be helped to care for themselves. The objective being improved self-help, it would be difficult to argue that the investigator should try to avoid influencing the situation for the better, although the result might then be a lack of generality of conclusion. A more important problem is that some investigators have used the term 'action research' as an alternative to formulating research objectives. There is no excuse for this and we must reject such approaches although, unfortunately, they have occurred widely in health care developments. It would be less erroneous to label such activities simply as 'innovations' rather than as 'experiments' or 'action research' or 'demonstration projects'. Presumably the use of such terms as 'experiment' and 'action research' has facilitated the diversion of research resources and this explains their vogue. The result in many cases has been waste of research and development resources on an enormous scale in such areas as the use of computers in health care work and in the development of complex screening regimes.

11.9. USE OF MODELS

The concept of a model is fundamental to scientific philosophy, and models are used as conceptual and as practical tools in both the natural and the social sciences, including medicine and epidemiology.

A model is easier to define in terms of what it does than in terms of what it is. A model is a conceptual, symbolic, or physical object or system which *represents* some 'real' object or system; it represents it in the sense that observations or experiments relating to the model provide an understanding or prediction of events or effects in the 'real' case. The argument is by analogy, to the extent that if the analogy is seen to break down, the model is no longer regarded as valid. Cause–effect relationships may be regarded as *conceptual* models. They are inferred on the basis of data which were observed in the past and are used as a model for the future. The notion of a 'disease' may also be regarded as a model, a composite concept of a process representing a group of sick people and expressed partly in words, partly in numerical probabilities (e.g. of prognosis), and partly in terms of sets of micro-photographs, epidemiological graphs, cardiographic traces, or other analogue material. Indeed, the whole point of making diagnoses in clinical medicine hinges upon the idea of a disease being a model. The act of diagnosis then brings into play a wide range of additional information not contained within the findings of the history, examination, and investigation of the individual patient. This is of vital importance to the patient's clinical care.

Certain classes of model are peculiar to the epidemiological approach. Together, they almost define it. They include transmission models, related chiefly to the infectious diseases. However, transmission models can be applied also to mental disorders, drug addictions, or levels of demand upon health care services. The model of an interaction between agent, host, and environment is widely used in analysing infective and toxic disorders. However, it too can be enlarged to encompass behavioural, nutritional, occupational, and other kinds of disorder. Cause-and-effect models, while not peculiar to the epidemiological approach, frequently assume a format which differs from those more frequently understood in clinical practice, in physiological studies, and in laboratory experiments. The difference is enshrined in the use of two technical terms, 'aetiology' and 'pathogenesis'. The aetiology of a disease or disability consists of the postulated web of causes which *precedes* it, and whose interruption might lead to its prevention. Pathogenesis is concerned with the postulated mechanisms of the pathological process itself, providing an explanation of the way in which the clinical features depend upon the underlying histopathological or morbid anatomical or biochemical abnormalities. These mechanisms are contained within the disease process itself, constitute part of its definition, and are of a special interest to therapists who hope to interrupt or modify one or more of the stages.

Epidemiologists who become involved in health care planning tend to adopt and use different models from those employed by epidemiologists concerned with the maintenance of health and the prevention of disease. It is in their habitual repertoire of models, rather than in their basic techniques, that they tend most to differ. Since operational models pure and simple (e.g. queues, waiting lists, transport, staffing structures, etc.) are the special prerogative of operational research (operations research) specialists, the epidemiologist will be especially concerned with those models in which operational and biological considerations interact. Frameworks for studying and representing screening procedures for hypertension, cervix cancer, and for childhood developmental surveillance, are all of this type. Such models will almost always include social/behavioural components, as well as means of representing natural histories and the effectiveness of treatment, and many will include aspects of the economics of the service.

One other feature characterizes the model framework of the epidemiologist/planner as compared with the epidemiologist pursuing problems of disease causation. His models tend to be not simply a structured explanation of observed facts, but also working tools. Many of them are expressed in mathematical terms and some of them form the basis of simulation systems carried out on computers. A good case can be made out that, whereas human beings can handle a limited number of variables quite efficiently in simple intuitive terms and can come up with the right answers, complex situations with more than a few variables are beyond their comprehension, and their intuitive conclusions are often demonstrably wrong. Many of the social/economic/biological/operational models on which projections of complicated policies must be based, are too complicated for reliance upon intuitive approaches, at least in any quantitative sense. Certainly they are too complex for rational verbal discussion without a good deal of analytical and numerical support. For working models whose validity cannot be checked on intuitive grounds, it is important that they be 'validated' by checking their predictions through mimicking real life situations whose consequences are known, or can be discovered.

In contexts where there is argument, and in health care planning there often is, there are considerable advantages in having the bases of a projection explicit, with the facts, the method of computation, and the arithmetic itself, recognizable as separate issues. This serves to localize the basis of any disagreement and to introduce a higher level of rationality. Mathematical and computer simulation models are still specialist techniques, and more suitable for complex planning problems than for simple ones, but they probably point the way to the future and epidemiologists must expect to play their part in their formulation and application.

12. Epidemiological approaches to planning

In Chapter 11 we described the techniques and the conceptual background of the epidemiological approach, and we noted that there were variations in emphasis according to the context of its application. This was reflected in a varied technical repertoire, but the main difference between the preventive and biological fields on the one hand, and the health care field on the other, lay in the model frameworks employed. This is because epidemiology is a problem-orientated discipline and the detailed approaches employed by its practitioners depend upon the problems with which they are faced.

This principle applies equally to the different levels and the different conditions of health care planning itself, and the different degrees to which epidemiological skills are accepted or available. Where epidemiologists are excluded from the planning mechanism they are limited to the use of observational techniques to study effectiveness and standards, and have little incentive to undertake predictive work or to participate in the construction of operational models. Their access to information is limited, they have to employ such data as they can obtain, and they have little opportunity to contribute to the structure and management of the internal information services of the health care system. This is in contrast with the functions and interests of epidemiologists who participate in all parts of the planning cycle. Even for the latter group, however, there will be variations of emphasis according to the level of planning in which they are involved.

In Chapter 12 we shall describe the different kinds of problems which epidemiologists meet, mainly through a series of illustrations. We shall follow the sequence of the planning cycle as laid out in Part I and shall illustrate each part of it. Thus, as it were, we are assuming that the working relationship of the epidemiologist is fully integrated with the planning cycle, and that the epidemiologists themselves are familiar with the full range of technique necessary for this role. We are aware that in many real situations this integration does not exist, and in these contexts the illustrations may be treated as examples of lost opportunities.

Our presentation has a secondary purpose. The systematized

picture of planning processes presented in Part I creates an un-realistic impression of order and simplicity. Although we hope that our examples will illustrate that the idealized representation of a cyclical process is generally valid and that epidemiological techniques have a place in each part of it, they will also demonstrate the complex and untidy ways in which the cycle operates in real life. Thus, although situation analysis is shown at a particular part of the figurative cycle, the theme recurs repeatedly in each of a series of sub-cycles associated with every one of the main steps. A further (and recurrent) situation analysis is required in designing an operational plan, as well as at the points shown in Fig. 1. Value systems also enter at both places, although at the more general level they are likely to be concerned with questions of equity and of general priori-ties, and at the second level with such issues as professional division of labour and the confidentiality and security of records.

We shall for the purposes of this section begin at the top of the cycle given in Fig. 1 and proceed through situation analysis and its translation to the formulation and choice of priorities; then to the formulation and elaboration of objectives; next to the formulation of different means to these ends, the prediction of outcomes, and the choice between alternatives; next to the setting up of operational plans together with the means of monitoring the implementation, and, where necessary, the conduct of pilot studies and experiments; next to the process of implementing the plan and collecting the data on which current monitoring and subsequent evaluation can be based; finally to the process of definitive evaluation and its effect upon all the other parts of the cycle.

12.2. SITUATION-ANALYSIS PROBLEMS

Pressures to change services arise from dissatisfaction with the present state of affairs, whether this be in the negative sense that the present is patently unacceptable, or in the more constructive sense that a better alternative has been envisaged. The idea of 'need', discussed in § 8.2, is central to this process.

The perception, formulation, and reformulation of medical needs by planners is a continuing process and one to which a range of professional contributions is necessary. The contributors include economists, sociologists, politicians, professional-group represen-tatives, clinicians, managers, and epidemiologists. However, since the sickness, health, and needs of populations and the measure of the effectiveness of services, are described and defined largely in epidemiological terms, it must follow that the epidemiological con-tribution is essential and even paramount. This is independent of whether a professional epidemiologist supplies it.

An example of epidemiological participation in the definition of health care need is supplied in a report sponsored by the Health Commission of New South Wales, Australia (Gwynne 1975) on the subject *Indicators of needs for use in health service planning*. During the early 1970s, as a result of political pressures, a large amount of money was channelled into a 'community health programme' with special emphasis on 'primary care'. In order to ensure that this money was spent in the most appropriate way a requirement arose for a method of indicating which communities were in greatest need of new services. A number of indicators were developed and examined. They included doctor-to-patient ratios, bed-to-population ratios, population age/sex characteristics, socio-economic characteristics, employment statistics, social problem indicators (e.g. proportion of migrants), observed shortages of general practitioners, nurses, dentists, etc., geographical distances from emergency care departments, inadequate access to ambulances and hospital beds, and others. The investigation was designed to monitor the geographical distribution of medical care provision, rather than modify or measure the effectiveness of care, and was based upon the premise that provision was an end in itself.

Whereas *this* Australian example was based entirely upon available sources of data, other studies have required supplementary special investigations and sample surveys. They have included the assembly of felt needs as expressed in demand, and usage as determined through interview and studies of utilization of existing health services, and expenditure (Abel-Smith 1967; Fry and Farndale 1972).

A situational analysis with a more specific 'output orientation' was reported from India. In the period 1953–4 about 75 million of the 360 million population were affected by malaria, and it killed about 0·8 million each year. It accounted for over 10 per cent of hospital and dispensary visits and the child parasite-rate was 4 per cent. The disease was responsible for large economic losses in the agricultural and industrial sectors.

The epidemiological investigation of this problem passed through several stages. The first provided the general characterizations laid out above and singled out the problem for special attention. It stimulated a major attempt to reduce the incidence of malaria through the 'National Malaria Control Programme', established in 1953 (Dy 1954). The basic strategy depended mainly upon control of the vector, and the large-scale use of residual insecticides. In the course of monitoring this programme the situation changed and a new analysis was required. The first new problem was the emergence of insecticide resistance in the vector and the second was the realization that the control programme was expensive and was likely to remain so for the indefinite future. The new situation created by these observations required a decision as to whether attempts should be made to eradicate the disease. This would be even more expensive in the short run but preferable on all other grounds provided that it was successful. The decision to proceed was taken in 1958 and the programme was planned for completion in 1968–9, but setbacks imposed revisions and extensions. From 1965 onwards the incidence began to increase rather than decrease, and by 1973 the cost of the programme was several *times* the planned expenditure. Cash shortage, an overextended resource for carrying out spraying operations, an increasing incidence, and a shortage of insecticides, have made a new situational analysis urgently necessary.

Another example of an output-related problem is reported from Canada (Meyer *et al.* 1975) where solution of the problem of low birth weight was seen to be crucial to further reductions of perinatal mortality. Socio-economic status, race, parity, maternal age, maternal height, and maternal weight have been repeatedly demonstrated to be associated with low average birth weight and with a high proportion of low-birth-weight infants. Low birth weight has been shown repeatedly to be associated with high stillbirth and high neonatal death rates, high rates of physical and mental disability, and high and costly demands upon the medical care services. The *effects* of low birth weight can be inferred with some certainty, but its *causes* are less clear.

However, one probable causal element was recently demonstrated; tobacco smoking during pregnancy substantially reduces birth weight. The mechanism is probably through an effect upon the state of the placenta. Meyer *et al.* (1976) have shown that placenta previa and abruptio placenta are more frequent among women who smoke during pregnancy, even after adjustment for other factors influencing the risk of these placental complications. However, we cannot be entirely certain that the associations are not partly indirect, and due to unrecognized underlying factors (e.g. nutritional); an experimental or quasi-experimental approach therefore seems to be called for. It would take the form of a preventive experiment carried out on a large scale and mediated through health educational methods with adequate monitoring of effectiveness. The planning problem is recognized as one of imposing a large-scale experiment upon a service situation, which would require the co-operation of a very large number of service personnel.

A need whose perception arose from the results of an epidemiological investigation is reported from Australia (McMichael and Hetzel

1974a, b). The investigation was designed to test the validity of a method through which university students could be helped to make a self-assessment with respect to mental illness. The method was developed, examined, found to be reproducible, and found to correlate well with established neuroticism scores. However, it also revealed varying but significant severities of disturbance in 38 per cent of first year students and 49 per cent of second year students and the findings were strongly correlated with examination performance and with the risk of subsequent withdrawal from the university. The investigation therefore revealed and quantified the extent of a need for professional help. It created a problem for medical care planners and at the same time indicated the manner in which it might be solved.

Situational analyses guided by epidemiological investigation sometimes point the way to a series of alternative solutions rather than a unique proposal. Another Australian example illustrates this point. It arose from a requirement that emergency care departments in metropolitan Sydney should be staffed and equipped in a rational way. The investigation was based upon a study of the types and levels of demand placed upon existing departments throughout the Metropolitan area. All patients during a two-week period were characterized according to their source, the types of operations carried out, and the levels of medical and nursing skills employed or required. The skills were shown to be similar to those required for other kinds of services and already combined in a variety of existing units. This permitted formulation of a series of options from which the planners could choose. Such plans could not have been developed without a full enquiry into existing demands, existing resources, related services, and projections relating to all three.

The integral nature of such enquiries was emphasized in a WHO (European Regional Office) publication on *Health planning and organization of medical care* (1972) which stated. . .'Increasing funds or manpower will increase the total resources available, but can never increase them to a level such that all potential demands can be met. It is thus always necessary to ask two different questions. First, what total resources can be made available for health? Second, how should those resources be allocated to the various competing needs? The answer to the second question can *never* be avoided by any *realistic* answer to the first.'

12.3. PRIORITIES AND OBJECTIVES

The situational analyses exemplified in § 12.2 lead rationally towards decisions about priorities, but not without a forward glance. Priority decisions are based only partly upon the pressures of the situation and require also an assessment of the feasibility of alternative solutions. Question of feasibility demand that general objectives are resolved and elaborated into precise behaviourally-expressed components. This is necessary as much for a prior evaluation of *likely* outcome as it is for an eventual *post hoc* evaluation of *actual* success or failure. Thus, the setting of priorities and the formulation of objectives are indissolubly linked in the planning cycle. They require judgement, knowledge, and wisdom, and an ability to synthesize numerous details in different dimensions.

Formulating objectives is a time-consuming task. In addition to declaring the main intended outputs, they should define the data needed to evaluate the system. A set of intermediate operational objectives will have to be laid out covering financial requisitions, the obtaining of agreements, the setting out of alternative strategies if obstructions should be encountered, the whole being incorporated within a timetable. For complex plans it is necessary to construct a detailed 'critical path' strategy. Objectives are variously set in terms of the provision of care, the effect upon health status of that provision, the standards of care to be attained, or the minimum standards to be maintained in the face of reduced resources. Complex problems require the elaboration of sub-plans with sub-objectives, and priority choices will occur within the total programme as well as between the programme and alternative courses of action.

Typical examples may be found in many parts of the world in relation to the care of elderly people. Rising populations of aged infirm are exerting pressures upon a limited capacity to care for them in hospitals, in nursing homes, or in residential homes for the aged. The situation requires that two general objectives should be adopted, first, to provide more residential places and, second, to provide domiciliary support services which might reduce the demand upon them. The first objective disaggregates naturally into several components including the provision of new buildings, the discharge from hospital of patients who do not need hospital, and a reduction of costs of those who are in hospital through ensuring that they do not occupy facilities more heavily serviced than a reasonable standard of care demands. The second general objective disaggregates into a requirement that the critical determinants of admission to institutional care should be identified and that domiciliary support services to ameliorate these problems be provided, also into a requirement for preventive surveillance, both medical and social, so that critical episodes can be forestalled, also into a requirement for the provision of suitable housing and living conditions, so that institutional care is less likely to become necessary. Each of these objectives will demand a sub-plan of its own, each with its planning mechanism.

Several studies, for example in Australia (Lefroy 1967; Lefroy and Page 1972) and the United Kingdom (Williamson *et al.* 1964; Shaw 1975) have demonstrated high rates of physical and functional disabilities in elderly populations living in their own homes, high levels of social isolation, and low levels of support from domiciliary health and social service agencies. Several studies (Cosin 1956; Exton-Smith 1962; McKeown and Cross 1969; Kisteen and Morris 1972; Smits *et al.* 1974; Bradshaw *et al.* 1976) have shown that for those elderly people in institutional care many are not in the situation best (and most economically) suited to meeting their needs. That is, there are many elderly people in hospitals who would be better in residential homes and many in the reverse situation, many in psychiatric hospitals who do not need psychiatric care, or in non-psychiatric hospitals or in residential homes, when they do in fact require psychiatric care. Some of those in hospital could be discharged if more attention were paid to supporting services in the community, while others are being maintained at home in circumstances (or at costs) suggesting that they would be better off in hospital.

There are many obstructions to putting these matters right. In many countries the administrative responsibilities for supportive community services, residential homes, nursing homes, and different kinds of hospitals, are separate. A realistic setting of objectives here, must often begin with an administrative reorganization such that an overall responsibility can be localized and an appropriate authority over combined resources declared. So far as community support services are concerned a first objective will often have to be stated in terms of increased inputs of resources, but even with improvements the deployment of these resources cannot be planned without detailed local information. For example, in the United Kingdom, an investigation was carried out (Shaw 1975) of the logistics (timings, mileages, numbers of visits per day) of providing surveillance of elderly people using nurses. It was then shown that existing domiciliary nursing resources in the country as a whole would not be sufficient to meet this requirement even if the whole resource could be assigned to this single task. Frequent universal geriatric surveillance was therefore shown to be an unrealistic objective and the question then arose whether selective visiting could meet a major part of the need and whether a sufficiently selective group of criteria could be devised. Here again, the realism of an objective stated in these terms will depend upon the outcome of specific investigation.

Objectives need to be reset repeatedly for various reasons. One (as in the geriatric surveillance example) arises when a first objective is shown to be impracticable. Objectives may be discovered (afterwards) to have been impracticable from the beginning. Alternatively (as in the malaria control example) the situation changes, and the objective *becomes* impracticable. In other situations a first objective is in fact achieved and a sequence of new objectives have to be devised.

The history of smallpox control in India, and its subsequent eradication, provides an example in this last class. The first objective, was for a higher level of 'control' through the medium of a mass vaccination campaign, and an immediate target was to achieve 80 per cent vaccination in all sections of the population within three years. It was assumed that the immunity level thus achieved would be sufficient to interrupt many, if not all, chains of smallpox transmission. A second level objective was also identified. It was intended that once the 80 per cent target had been achieved in all sections and all age groups of the population, an adequate immunity level could be maintained by vaccinating all newborns and revaccinating children at the ages two, five, ten, and fifteen years, together with all contacts of every smallpox patient.

As the programme progressed it was found that the first target could not be reached in three years, also that smallpox continued to spread even in areas with 80 per cent coverage. However, the incidence was reduced sufficiently to bring a new objective within reach, namely regional eradication. Three new operational objectives were declared and acted upon, namely:

(1) The setting up of an active surveillance system capable of detecting all new smallpox outbreaks quickly;
(2) The epidemiological investigation of all outbreaks;
(3) Institution of containment measures for all detected outbreaks.

To meet these objectives additional sources of information were recruited through civic leaders, school teachers, and school children. Cash awards were announced for the first persons informing about previously unreported smallpox outbreaks in certain areas. Setbacks continued to occur, particularly where intensive searching revealed that there were still many more cases than those which had been reported (Henderson 1976). However, continued efforts reduced the incidence to the point where total eradication was seen to be attainable, and this target—'Operation Target Zero'—was adopted in July 1973. The last case occurred on 24 May 1975 and the country was declared to be smallpox-free by the International Commission in April 1977 (WHO, 1978a, b).

One further fact which sometimes determines the appropriateness of an objective, and sometimes requires it to be reset, is the more realistic appraisal of the power network which the planning operation serves. For example, Regional Health Authorities in England were made responsible for local medical manpower planning. For health purposes, England is the sum of its fourteen regions, and every region has one or more medical schools. In practice, however, the future supply of doctors is determined by the output of all the schools of the country taken together as well as by immigration and emigration, and so in fact no Regional Health Authority acting alone has control over supply. The result has been that regional manpower planning activities have concentrated almost entirely upon the question of demand—the question of how many doctors will be needed in the light of changing standards, changing population sizes, and changing population structures. Even here, however, the critical constraint is not so much a projection of perceived needs as the availability of central finance, which is determined by central government. Thus, regional manpower planning became detached from the seat of the necessary powers and proved to be an exercise of very limited value. In this case the proper solution is a relocation of manpower planning responsibilities, a change which has recently been accepted and acted upon.

It is only at the level of detailed implementation and evaluation, that the adequacy or inadequacy of preset objectives becomes assessable. General goals, although necessary, seldom lend themselves to accurate appraisal before these detailed stages have been reached and many, in practice, prove to be inconsistent, unattainable, non-evaluable, or to contain large gaps. An investigation carried out by the U.S. Department of Health, Education, and Welfare (1976)— *Base lines for setting health goals and standards*',—analysed the stated health goals of 48 countries. The goals varied widely, but very few of a range of suggested health status indicators were consistently used as objectives. Twenty-three of the 48 countries wished to 'reduce communicable disease' and 14 to 'reduce infant mortality'; besides these, only 15 other health status objectives were cited. So far as *provision* of health services was concerned the most frequently stated objectives were to 'increase access in rural and urban areas' (25), 'increase the number of providers' (24), 'increase the number of facilities' (23), and 'improve maternal and child health services' (20). All of these outcomes were likely to occur in any case, whether there was realistic planning or not. Comprehensive general plans were quoted from Canada, the United Kingdom, Sweden, West Germany, U.S.S.R., Mexico, and the countries of South America (via the Pan

American Health Organization). The United States itself (from which the analysis comes) has also expended considerable effort on the construction of national and area comprehensive health plans. This limited analysis of the world scene concludes that most countries have *not* in fact produced explicit statements of their nation's intentions in the health field. For some there is no clearly enunciated position and for others a plethora of statements, some duplicative and some conflicting. Some state their objectives in terms of seeking international aid and often concentrate on what has already been accomplished rather than future intentions. Many are 'seemingly unrealistic', calling for resources which do not exist and setting target dates which must be impossible to meet. There were 'obvious disparities' between what particular health plans said and how the country's health system was actually run, and there was often a lack of attention to updating health plans to take account of changing needs and changing political and social situations.

12.4. DECISIONS BETWEEN ALTERNATIVE TACTICAL PLANS

The formulation of objectives requires a forward look at a proposed plan of action. The choice of plan requires a forward look at a series of alternatives. Each must be examined in some detail and it is at this stage of the planning cycle, especially, that the planners need to conceive of the intended service as a system in order to analyse it, to forecast the way it will work, and to predict its outcomes. This exercise must be repeated for each of the main alternatives, for each of the detailed modifications to which each plan lends itself, and for a range of premises and assumptions designed to cover the factual uncertainties of the situation. Modelling techniques are used extensively for these purposes; indeed, this is the only possible way to proceed. If there is any choice it is not so much *whether* models will be used, but rather *what kinds* of models (Bailey 1975).

Since most planning is incremental, providing additional resources or redeploying existing resources and looking for *additional* benefits, it is necessary as a rule to make a base-line assessment of existing standards and performance. It is difficult to proceed without such an appraisal and this task is a special responsibility of epidemiologists. The task may have been accomplished in its 'proper place' in the evaluation phase of the planning cycle, but often it will be found that these investigations have been omitted, are not adaptable to the present task, or have become outdated in the course of time.

An example arose in the United Kingdom (Bywaters and Knox 1976) where the possibility was raised of introducing widespread screening for breast cancer, using palpation and mammography. It was suggested that the service be introduced on an experimental basis in selected regions as part of a scientifically controlled process of development. It was necessary to establish base-line conditions to discover (a) whether the traditional therapeutic service was performing sufficiently well to justify this expensive new measure—as opposed to the alternative of upgrading the service—, and (b) whether the existing service was sufficiently well organized to carry the superimposed experiment and its attendant control processes. An investigation was carried out based upon samples of breast cancer cases extracted from the cancer registry and the very simple data available established several important facts. First, waiting times at various stages of the referral and diagnostic processes were very variable and when the components were added together the total delays were often excessive. Not all of these delays could be attributed to the patients. Secondly, it was found that almost all surgeons in the region saw at least one case each year, but that more than half of them saw fewer than five cases each per year. Only two surgeons saw more than thirty cases per year. It appeared that lack of systemization may have been responsible for some part of the waiting times, not so much because the surgeons themselves were inexperienced, but because the many channels of the referral/diagnostic/therapeutic service were generally 'unlubricated' from disuse. It was considered unlikely, as a result of this investigation, that the existing service could provide the background for the proposed experimental one or that this would be the best deployment for additional funds.

It is sometimes necessary to estimate the upper limits of likely improvement as well as the base line from which the improvement must start. An example is reported by Opit and Crawford (1975) from the United Kingdom where a question arose relating to the staffing of the obstetric anaesthesia service. The issues related to the ratios between senior and junior staff, the allocation of nursing staff, the mode of allocating working sessions of anaesthetists to different hospitals, and the maintenance of equipment. The investigation established the base line through identifying describing, and counting all the disasters, mishaps, and near-mishaps in a defined region for a defined period of time. Since the 'output' objective was to eliminate these situations, the upper boundary of the intended benefit was also thus identified. Investigations succeeded in relating the risk of mishap to the level of investment and the methods of employment of staff and enabled the investigators to make relatively precise statements of the degree to which different defined reductions in hazard might be obtained from specific increments of investment and redeployments of duties. That is, these investigators succeeded in relating the resources of the service to its output standards.

Although the prime interest of the epidemiologist in such circumstances relates to biological variables such as natural history and effectiveness of treatment, he must also involve himself in the appraisal of technical issues. The assessment of error rates and of the replicability of medical investigations may be crucial to the way in which a plan is formulated and an objective adopted. This will apply, for example, where multiphasic screening procedures are adopted and where, as many health care services have learned to their costs, a combination of several bad tests makes a very bad test indeed. The definition and maintenance of technical standards extends also to the information systems on which epidemiological work so largely depends. This is shared responsibility, but one to which the epidemiologist must contribute.

Ethical standards, as well as technical standards, involve the epidemiologist in a shared responsibility. Questions of confidentiality will affect him when questions arise relating to the usage of clinical records for large-scale investigative purposes. Confidentiality can be seen from several points of view, and it goes beyond the identification of individual patients and the disclosure of clinical information about them. It is necessary often to avoid specific identification of small groups (e.g. villages, minorities), and also of doctors and nurses involved in providing medical care, and sometimes of medical institutions, or the regions served by them.

Decisions on confidentiality are not always easy and it has to be recognized that the corporate needs of societies are sometimes at conflict with the individual needs of their members (see Parts I and II). A fundamental insistence on *absolute* secrecy can be as *harmful* as an overriding concern with value to the community. From the first viewpoint it may appear illegitimate to transmit and use clinical information even when identities have been removed, because the information is being used for a purpose for which explicit prior consent was not given. A doctor with the needs of the population in mind is more likely to take the view that non-identifiable information may be used for the common good, and that there is an implied consent of the originator unless it was explicitly withheld. Most patients, and most doctors would probably take the latter point of view.

Ethical constraints upon alternative courses of action and upon alternative choices of objectives extend beyond the question of confidentiality. Another difficult area relates to proposals to carry out experiments upon human beings. The scientific attractions of experimentation were discussed in Chapter 11, but the ethical problems can be formidable. First, all epidemiologists would agree that it is necessary to be frank with patients before inviting them to take part in a trial in which they would be randomly allocated to different groups, but problems may arise where, for one reason or another, the patient is unable to give explicit and competent consent. Examples arise in devising alternative methods of care (e.g. hospital admission versus home care) for mentally sick patients, or for those who are sufficiently sick to be incapable of a rational appreciation of the request made of them. Patients with a severe attack of coronary thrombosis or incapable of speech (e.g. with stroke) are physically incapable of giving consent. In the case of children it is usually the parents who give consent, but there is both a legal and a moral problem here; are they in fact competent to do so?

In all these problems there is an intractable incompatibility between two alternative and fundamentalist points of view and the only reasonable recommendation that can be made—it can scarcely be called a solution—is that judgement must be exercized. Often it must be a shared judgement but one to which epidemiologists and, especially, medically qualified epidemiologists, may be expected to contribute.

'Forward look' operations go beyond the identification of base-line situations and of technical, ethical, and resource constraints. They include specific attempts to predict the consequences of alternative policies. The planner has to be a forecaster, and he is faced with a pair of axioms, namely that (1) all rational decisions depend upon predictions, and (2) all rational predictions depend upon models. Planning must therefore depend upon models, whether intuitive or explicit and it is especially in relation to explicit models that the epidemiologist's skills will be marshalled (see Chapter 11). Sometimes he will contribute to model formulations which are chiefly the responsibility of other workers (e.g. operational research workers), but sometimes he will have to develop them himself. To a considerable extent he will have to develop the habits of mind and the methods of the systems analyst. This developing theme is described in a text edited by Bailey and Thompson (1975) describing a programme of studies developed by the International Institute of Applied Systems Analysis (IIASA).

An example of an approach to a problem through the construction of a systems model was reported by Knox (1973). It concerned the detailed deployment, or redeployment, of the cervical cytology screening service in the United Kingdom. At the time of the investigation the service was providing about 2 000 000 cervical smears per year for a population at risk of about 16 000 000 women aged 20 to 65. The current policy, arrived at empirically, was that screening should begin at about age 35 and be repeated at five-year intervals, although there were exceptions for high parity women who would be screened at earlier ages. The policy was encouraged by the terms of additional payments to general practitioners for taking smears at the appropriate ages but the policy was not closely followed in practice and many smears were performed in younger women and often repeated annually. Pressures developed to modify the policy in the direction of current practice, through providing additional payments for smears in the younger women. Estimates of the effectiveness of the alternative policies hinged partly upon estimates of the natural history of cervical pathologies, including the tempo of progression and the probability of progression and the way these factors vary with age. Positive and negative error rates and their variation with age are also relevant, as are levels of acceptability at different ages and in different social groups. None of these things is known with certainty.

The problem was approached first through analysing and briefly presenting the problem in these terms and secondly through devising a graphical method for predicting the effects of the simpler alternatives. The graphical method was subsequently converted to a computer programme in order to improve convenience of usage and to permit a wider range of options to be examined. Finally, an iterating version of the programme was constructed so that alternative policies could be tested in relation to different assumptions about the factual uncertainties. It was shown that for a wide range of assumptions, and within the range of currently available and foreseeably available resources, the largest and most immediate returns were obtained through concentrating upon the older women (ages 35 and over) rather than upon the younger ones. In this case, it seems that the intuitive model on which the early policy was based could be supported on the basis of a more formal approach. Formal approaches have the additional advantage that they separate quite clearly any arguments which there might be about the factual premises and assumptions, about the range of policy options which were in fact tried out, and about the accuracy of arithmetic.

Models of these kinds can contain economic as well as biological and operational components or are capable of interpretation in economic terms. It is not our purpose to expound principles of health economics in this text, but we may note that many of the concepts used by health economists are identical with those used by epidemiologists working in the health care planning field. They relate to inputs and outputs, budgetary costs, and alternative economic costings, to the balance between investment now and (discounted) benefit later or between capital and revenue expenditures, and to marginal returns for marginal investments. Epidemiologists and economists will agree that economic principles and methods are useful aids towards achieving the objectives of health care services. We hope they will also agree that while cash accounting may be employed towards these ends, it should not mistakenly be used as the basis for setting the goals.

12.5. IMPLEMENTATION, INNOVATION, AND EXPERIMENT

Implementation of proposed changes in the output of the planning cycle. This is the stage during which the management function dominates, and in which epidemiologists and other scientists play a relatively small part. This is partly traditional and partly for sound practical reasons. However, it is important to remember that this is part of the planning cycle, and not separate from it, and that the scientific role is not entirely extinguished. Indeed, the strength of the management activity, here, makes it all the more important to be clear about the exact role of the epidemiologist so that he is not simply swept up in the drive of management activities.

His two main legitimate concerns are with (1) the concomitant establishment of the information system which will later permit him to assess the effectiveness of the changes, and (2) in circumstances where a definitive form of service cannot be determined from the beginning, with the design and conduct of experiments and pilot implementations to guide subsequent decisions. In both respects it can be seen that he is concerned especially with change at a second level, that is, not simply with the changes accomplished through implementation of the initial plan, but with future changes in the plan itself. Both the manager and the epidemiologist require a degree of 'control' for different purposes. The working relationship is necessarily difficult and it will colour the discussions to be presented in Part IV of this book. The 'information' interests of the epidemiologist are associated with the monitoring and evaluation exercises appropriate to later parts of the planning cycle and to later sections of this book. In this chapter we shall limit ourselves to an exploration of experimental involvements.

An example is provided by developments taking place in several parts of the world with respect to the care of patients suffering from acute coronary occlusion. There has been a greatly increased provision of special hospital units for these patients. Their initial justification was based upon the observation that, since intensive care had to be provided in any case, it was probably more economical in staff and other resources to concentrate this care in particular locations. This raised the standards of care provided, engendered enthusiasms on the part of the staffs involved, and attracted investment in equipment. This was also accompanied by a shift in the implied objectives. That is, it became widely believed that case-fatality rates were substantially reduced and this belief, in turn, has raised a general policy problem. There is of course an obvious trap in the interpretation made, in that growth of a specialized facility will widen the range of clientele. Less severe cases will be accommodated and result in an improved average prognosis. In some places, however, for example in Australia, there has also been a noticeable decline in population mortality from myocardial infarction and there may be some substance in the more optimistic claims, although other explanations could be advanced. The question now arises as to how much additional investment is justified in new units, technical equipment, and staff training. The potential costs are very large indeed; how large are the benefits? (Chapman 1970; Robinson and McLean 1970; Etheridge 1971; Pole 1972).

In this planning problem, the 'pilot experiment' was not centrally planned but arose from initiatives at the periphery and the problem was thrust upon central administrative authorities rather than deliberately adopted by them. Nevertheless, formal trials have subsequently been planned or implemented both in Australia and in the United Kingdom and the results are providing guidance towards a more rational development of policy. Mather et al. (1971, 1976) studied 450 patients with suspected myocardial infarctions and without hypotension or complicating circumstances, and they were randomly allocated to one of two groups. One group was admitted to hospital and the other group treated at home. Assessments were made at 28 days and at 330 days. The home care group had a slightly lower fatality rate than the hospital group. Investigation was of course limited to those patients in whom the prognosis was assessed as relatively good, and the findings give little guidance concerning outcomes in more severe cases, but the results set useful limits upon the extent to which intensive care might have to be provided, and the extent to which it might reduce mortality.

Policy for treating tuberculosis in India was subjected to analogous scientifically controlled development (Indian Council of Medical Research 1959; WHO 1960, 1964; Kamat et al. 1966). In the early 1950s there were 2·1 million cases of tuberculosis, only 23 000 tuberculosis beds, and a 'waiting-list' of about 100 cases per bed. This discrepancy could not be reduced in the short term and it was necessary to discover the extent to which simple domiciliary chemotherapy services could compare, in terms of effectiveness, with care provided in sanatoria. A controlled comparison was therefore carried out at a tuberculosis chemotherapy centre in Madras. The results showed that domiciliary care was practical and effective, had social advantages, and was safe for close family contacts.

Another example of a 'midstream' evaluative study is reported from the United States where Gordis (1973) enquired into the effectiveness of comprehensive care clinics in reducing the incidence of rheumatic fever. It was not a randomized study, but by comparing different census tracts on a 'before and after' basis, it was possible to show that the incidence of rheumatic fever had been reduced by about 60 per cent in those tracts served by well organized comprehensive care clinics over a period of four years.

Acceptability and compliance are major problems in the development of a service. Martin (1964) studied the response of patients to consultation and advice provided in a hospital out-patient clinic following referral there by a family physician. The patients were randomly divided into two groups. The patients in one group were verbally instructed to return to their family doctor within a stated period, while those in the other group were given written appointment slips. For the second group a random half of the referring physicians were given a copy of the appointment slip. The results, after two weeks, showed that the patients with written instructions returned for advice on 85 per cent of occasions, compared with 15 per cent among the others, but that provision of an appointment slip to the doctor himself did not have any additional effect.

Investigations of different ways of using staff are also susceptible to experimental approaches. An example from Canada (Spitzer *et al.* 1974) concerned the problem of substituting nurse-practitioners for physicians in primary care practice. Before-and-after comparisons were made in two groups of randomly allocated patients, and the final outcome showed that there were no subsequent differences in mortality experience or in physical functional capacity, nor were there any social or emotional differences. The quality of care was also found to be similar. In economic terms the nurse-practitioner substitution was favourable when viewed from the point of view of the costs incurred by the total society, but in budgetary terms the scheme was disadvantageous to the doctors (who employed the nurse-practitioners) because of restrictions on reimbursement. This was a situation where budgetary arrangements were less than optimal from the point of view of delivering economic health care, and where a change might be recommended.

Before leaving the topic of inter-current experimental evaluation, we should mention a general problem of control which has not yet been solved. This arises typically when a large-scale innovation, such as the introduction of expensive equipment, so influences the pattern of practice that it becomes impossible to withdraw it when the experimental period is over. To this extent the results of the evaluation become irrelevant, at least locally. Examples include the provision of computers in hospitals or of automated biochemistry or radio therapy equipments, and experiments which involve the restructuring of premises or the specialized redeployment of personnel. The last two tend to go together and occur, for example, in developments of mental health care where large 'chronic' hospitals are progressively emptied and replaced by day-care and short-term hospital accommodation, supported by social and domiciliary services. There have been several examples of innovations designed to evaluate the effectiveness of routine multiple biochemical screening of all patients admitted to hospital. Prior expectations have included the hoped-for result that hospital stays would be shortened, diagnostic accuracy improved, and the quality of care enhanced. Some of these experiments have been carried out on a simple before-and-after basis while others have allocated different levels of service on a randomized basis to different parts of a hospital. Almost uniformly the results have been (a) that there were no demonstrable differences; (b) that the absence of results may have been due to other constraints beyond the control of investigators, such as the visiting patterns of physicians; and finally (c) that despite the indeterminate outcome, the service had become so firmly entrenched in the hospital concerned that it could not now be discontinued.

12.6. EXTENDED MONITORING AND DATA-COLLECTION

Data acquisition and monitoring processes differ from the approaches described in the last section, both in terms of their tempo and their expectations. They tend to be relatively long-term, low-level activities rather than intensive, and are frequently observational rather than experimental and manipulative. They often take place against the general expectation that no action will need to be taken unless something unexpected occurs. These expectations are frequently disappointed.

Routine national health statistics form one basis for monitoring activities of these kinds. It was noticed in Australia during the 1960s that a striking rise in the suicide rate had occurred, especially in women. The rise was almost entirely due to suicide due to drug overdose. A secondary set of monitoring data was then brought into play, namely the national levels of prescribed drugs (including sedatives) assembled in connection with the government subsidy scheme operating under the Pharmaceutical Benefits Act. It was shown that the rise in suicides was associated with a striking rise in the prescribing of barbiturates during the 1960s. This followed introduction of a provision whereby up to 200 barbiturate tablets could be prescribed at one time in order to save the cost of a subsequent visit for a repeat prescription. The level of prescribing reached a maximum in 1967 when it was decided to impose a restriction of not more than 30 tablets at a single visit. This was followed by a sharp fall in the amount prescribed, and subsequently, of the suicide rate (Hetzel 1971; Oliver and Hetzel 1972, 1973).

Similar studies, using national statistics from a variety of countries, detected a rise in mortality from asthma during the period 1959–66. (Speizer *et al.* 1968a, b). The rise occurred at different times in different countries and was subsequently shown to be associated with widespread usage of certain kinds of aerosol inhalers. Subsequent discontinuation of these inhalers was followed by a fall in the mortality rates. With the increasing importance of the ill effects of drugs, many countries have now ceased to rely upon the *post hoc* recognition of large-scale drug disasters, and central routine systems for the recording of ill effects are now widely used.

There are, of course, many other examples of situations where the identification of a specific problem has led to the setting up of a specific rather than a general monitoring process. One example from Tasmania concerns a programme of goitre prevention in school children through the provision of supplementary iodine. The preventive treatment consisted of the administration of a tablet containing 10 mg potassium iodide each week through the schools. The monitoring process showed that the incidence of goitres in school fell gradually between 1949 and 1965 but that the fall was not uniform, and between 1960 and 1965 there was no change in three out of the seven regions. These failures were correlated with a lack of co-operation by individual schools and so a new strategy was developed. Iodization of bread was introduced in March 1966 and this was followed by a prompt further fall in the goitre rate. However, as further monitoring showed, the universal provision of supplementary iodine to populations which had been previously deprived of the element, was followed by an increased incidence of thyrotoxicosis in the over-40s (Clements *et al.* 1968; Stanburg *et al.* 1974; Trikojus 1974).

Another preventive service which was subject to continued monitoring was a childhood surveillance system in the United Kingdom based upon the establishment of registers of infants assessed to be 'at risk of handicap'. The registers themselves provided the source of the monitoring data and after some years of running several trends could be discerned. The first was that the proportion of children entered to the register had steadily risen and had reached levels (e.g. 35 per cent, typically) which compromised the objectives of the scheme. Secondly, it was noticed that the usage of the register was changing so that it was in fact an 'observation' register to which many children were entered *after* the handicap had been noticed, rather than on the grounds of a predefined risk. The question, therefore arose whether the 'at risk' register was meeting its initial needs, and this led to a series of definitive evaluations carried out in different parts of the country. One study in Birmingham (Knox and Mahon 1970) used a double approach, the first being based on a prospective study of the children identified as being 'at risk', and the other being based upon the retrospective study of patients subsequently identified as having a physical or educational handicap. The results of the two approaches were concordant and showed that although there were significant associations between the risk criteria and the occurrence of handicap, most of the handicapping conditions were not benefited or not likely to be benefited by early diagnosis and surveillance. It was also shown that the selectivity of the process was insufficient for operational purposes and that, if surveillance were to be carried out at all, there was no group from which it could reasonably be withheld. As a result of this and similar investigations the selective basis for childhood surveillance has now largely been abandoned.

Not all monitoring processes are related to outcome as in the last examples. Sometimes it is useful simply to monitor levels of activity in the service to ensure that operational objectives, at least, are being met. Many systems exist in different parts of the world for monitoring levels of hospital activity and of general practice activity, and they provide (usually) simple numerical statements of the numbers of patients seen, distributions by age and sex, distributions by diagnosis, by time of day, by day of week and by type of personnel. They have a rather limited application to health care planning but frequently provide a base line level so that the effects of administrative changes can be seen. An example in this class was reported by Munan *et al.* (1974) and McDonald *et al.* (1974) from Quebec, where the effect of a universal health insurance scheme upon the use of health services was examined. In this case there was no background information and the examination was based upon self-perceived utilization patterns elicited at interview ten months before and ten months after the health insurance plan came into effect. In fact there were no perceptible changes of usage.

12.7. EVALUATION

The process of evaluation closes the circle depicted in Fig. 1 and returns us to our arbitrary point of first entry, namely the situational analysis. That is, evaluation itself creates a new situation. It will, however, be understood by now, through reference to the examples given, that the phase of 'final evaluation' of the idealized cycle is entirely artificial. It would be difficult, for example, to support a rigorous separation of this stage from the stages of monitoring and of intercurrent evaluation, described in earlier sections. Every operation undertaken within health care planning contains an element of evaluation, in one of the several senses of that word. Every step in planning requires a forward look to the next step, as well as a backward look at the last one.

It might have been possible to admit at the outset that the epidemiological contribution to planning is basically evaluative, were it not for the danger that the term could be interpreted in too narrow a sense, and epidemiological activities limited to a narrow sector of an over-rigidly conceived cycle of activity. The cyclical model is not used solely in a conceptual sense, representing a fluid and dynamic system. In some health care services it has been made the basis of a time-tabled activity comprising 5-year plans at one level, shorter cycles at lower levels, and date-deadlines for time-tabling the interactions between the separate hierarchical layers. There is a good deal of sense and even of necessity in arrangements such as these, but the dangers of rigidity, of over-formalization, and of deleting some of the real complexity of a truly fluid system have to be recognized. The notion of a 'final evaluation' may therefore be dangerous as well as artificial and we have had some difficulty in choosing illustrative examples which can be conceived as 'end points'.

A simple study from Australia (Vulcan 1973) evaluated the effectiveness of the compulsory wearing of seat belts following legislation enacted in 1971 by the Victoria Government. First, there was an immediate increase in the wearing of seat belts from 25 per cent before the measure, to 75 per cent afterwards. Second, in the first nine months of 1971 there was a 17 per cent fall in road deaths and a 14 per cent fall in total road casualties among occupants of vehicles in Victoria, compared with small rises in other parts of Australia. The data not only justified the measure but resulted in other states adopting similar legislation.

A more complex evaluation of a service with narrowly defined objectives is examplified by studies of family planning programmes in India (Government of India 1974). Several family limitation techniques had been employed including conventional contraceptives, IUCD's, and male sterilization. First evaluations were carried out through converting the benefits to cash values and relating them to the costs of provision. Using these indices all methods gave high benefit–cost ratios, but they ranged from 3 : 1 for contraceptives to 18 : 1 for sterilization. There are obvious dangers in using evaluative methods such as these, arising from the arbitrariness both of the values assigned to each birth averted, and of the discount rate (10 per cent in this case) used for relating money spent 'now' to money saved 'later'.

A classical example of a service evaluation based upon a massive randomized controlled trial, was the investigation carried out by the Health Insurance Plan of New York (HIP), to determine the feasibility and measure the benefits and costs of breast cancer screening, using a combination of palpation and mammography (Shapiro *et al.* 1973). There were 31 000 women in each of two randomly allocated groups, only one of which received the screening service. Palpation and mammography were offered annually on four occasions and about 20 000 women in the 'treatment' group availed themselves of at least one test. Five years after the start of the experiment there had been 40 deaths from breast cancer in the screened group and 63 deaths in the control group, a difference of about one-third. This is probably the first unequivocal demonstration of the benefits of early diagnosis and treatment in this disease. Quantitatively the result is less encouraging than at first it seems, in that the number of deaths avoided represents only about 3 per cent of all the deaths which will be expected in a group of 31 000 women throughout their lifetimes. There is therefore a considerable gap between the circumstances demonstrated in the trial and those which would obtain if a more substantial proportion of total mortality were accepted as a service target. The process of extrapolating from experimental conditions to service conditions is a complex one which has been tackled through the use of computer models, and the results suggest that a target of 10 to 20 per cent reduction may be the most that can be reasonably hoped for without incurring prohibitive costs and prohibitive biopsy rates. Nevertheless, the HIP demonstration has placed service planners in a much more favourable position than they have ever been in relation to cervical cancer, for example.

A descriptive evaluation of mental health services (Wing and Hailey 1972) concerned the effects of the trend towards earlier discharge of patients from mental hospitals. These investigators described the nature of the problems which early discharge can create for the patient, his family, and the community. They found that the emotional health of the family may be seriously impaired by the strain of providing 24-hour vigilance over the patient, and for patients who spend much of their time in 'community hospitals' the situation may degenerate into neglect and even cruelty. There were also problems for patients in securing housing and employment. Costs to the hospital service were undoubtedly reduced but the monetary and non-monetary consequences outside the hospital, though more difficult to assess, may have been as great or even greater than those averted.

A major evaluative study relating to hospital care for the mentally handicapped has been described in West Sussex, England (Whitmore *et al.* 1975; Kushlick and McLachlan 1974, 1976). It was a matter of concern both to relatives of patients and to the Health Authority, to develop arrangements which were at once humane and constructive for the individuals involved, and least costly to the community. The methodological problems encountered related mainly to the development of evaluative criteria of performance and this in itself was a remarkable advance. The performance of the mentally handicapped can indeed be measured, as can improvements and deteriorations, and yet improvement or maintenance have seldom been accepted as serious evaluable objectives to be used by institutions caring for this kind of patient. Acceptance of these objectives involved the investigators in a long and complicated process of developing methods and standards, and the first results suggest that they are in fact practicable objectives and to some degree attainable. This study is an interesting example of what can be achieved by scientific application of epidemiological and statistical concepts in an imaginative way.

An investigation into the cost-effectiveness of health-care programmes for the treatment of drug abuse (Goldschmidt 1976) is another interesting approach in the same genre. Attention to the problems of measuring effectiveness and costs itself created standards which the personnel manning the services may not have initially accepted, not so much because they actively rejected them, but because they had never thought about them in this way before.

The investigations quoted above all have relatively narrow objectives and relate to 'functional' services, rather than 'institutional' services in the terms discussed in § 5.2. Many evaluation problems, however, relate to more complex services containing several different strands. Studies of multiple screening procedures (multiphasic screening) come into this class. They tend to be more difficult studies to carry out and to interpret because of the multiple components. That is, a 'negative' result may mask a mixture of beneficial, non-beneficial, and even harmful elements; a 'positive' evaluation may, on the other hand, be of little use because of the difficulty of knowing what to do next, whether to enhance the whole service, or part of it, and what part of it. A number of studies, some of them painstaking and carefully designed, have encountered problems of these kinds in relation to multiphasic screening (Cutler et al. 1973; Knox 1974; South-East London Screening Group 1977) and general guidance in these areas is still poor. It is becoming accepted, now, that two levels of evaluation are required, the one concerned with the individual components and the other with the benefits and problems of putting them together into an integrated scheme. The latter makes no sense without the former.

Some evaluative studies usefully concentrate upon patterns of utilization, although these investigations often have an 'interim' operational character. A well designed investigation of over-usage based upon long-term follow-up (five years) of matched controlled groups was carried out by the Kaiser–Permanente health plan. In particular, the management of over-usage was studied experimentally through comparing the effects of different psychological regimes. There were four groups treated at various levels (no psychotherapy, a single session, a brief course, and a long-term course) and the last three groups all showed significant declines in utilization of care services. The responses of the single-session and brief-course groups were quicker and more persistent than those of the long-term group. A related study demonstrated the reluctance of internists to refer patients for brief psychotherapy and the two studies together demonstrated objectively the nature of the problem, the potential benefits of intervention, and the obstacles to applying it (Follette and Cummings 1967; Cummings and Follette 1968).

In more complex cases still, evaluation becomes more explicitly concentrated upon the performance of institutions and Kessner and Kark (1973) have discussed strategies for researching these situations. Their solution is an interesting one in that it consists, in effect, of concentrating upon a selection of subsystems described in functional terms. Some of the examples they suggest for evaluating a comprehensive service include the care of middle ear infection and hearing loss, visual disorders, essential hypertension, urinary tract infections, and cervical cancer. They regard these functional services as 'tracers' for investigating the service as a whole, using isotope substitution studies as their analogy.

Problems of these kinds have arisen in recent years in relation to the performance of health centres in the United Kingdom, India, and elsewhere. In the United Kingdom the health centres are owned by the Health Authorities and occupied by general practitioners, who pay rent. General practitioners are not directly employed by the Health Authority but work alongside other staff who are so employed. The services provided include nursing services, health-visiting services, child welfare, dental, health education, family planning, and other activities. An alternative pattern of service is provided in many areas by groups of general practitioners working in new or modified premises which they themselves own. They receive low interest loans for modifying and maintaining these premises, and the supporting staff are employed directly by them, although they receive reimbursement. In practice the health centre approach is much more expensive than the group practice arrangement and the question arises to what extent the increased cost is reflected in an improved quality and range of services provided. Investigations have had to rely upon a disaggregation of this general question into a series of 'tracer' indicators including the quality of premises, the satisfaction of patients, the kinds of activities covered, the efficiency of use of personnel, and descriptions of the patterns of work of both doctors and nurses, referral and prescribing patterns, standards of accessibility at different times of day and on different days of the week, and so on.

Investigations of primary health centres in India, carried out by WHO, examined 139 such centres in seven different states of the country. It was found that only one case per thousand attendances was referred to hospital, only 10 per cent of the health centres had ever received a visit from a hospital consultant, and 70 per cent of the centres performed less than one laboratory test every second day. These simple figures showed that the centres work in considerable isolation and that there was a serious under-use of available resources (WHO 1966). A parallel study of the impact of local health services upon the rural population was based mainly upon data collected through village informants (Banagee 1974). The main findings were:

(a) That problems of medical care were regarded as by far the most urgent concern among the health problems of the rural population;
(b) There was discrimination against the poor with poor quality of care, lack of drugs, overcrowding, long waits, nepotism, bribery, and indifferent and often rude behaviour on the part of the staff;
(c) The local response to family planning was not very encouraging and indeed there was considerable antipathy. There were numerous complaints that villagers received no help when they encountered

complications following vasectomy, tubectomy, or IUCD in-
sertion;

(d) The supply of iron and folic acid tablets and of tetanus toxoid
injections for pregnant mothers, which were supposed to be
offered by the family planning programme, were virtually unknown
in the villages studied;

(e) The traditional birth attendants still conducted the majority
of deliveries, even in villages where health centres were located.

A happier example of the investigation of a complex service
through a study of its components came from Argentina where the
results of hospital treatment for nine paediatric diseases were studied.
The investigation was based upon four hospitals and 1500 children,
the children being divided evenly between the major teaching hospital
with high diagnostic and treatment standards and three hospitals
with basic standards. It was found on examination that the results of
treatment and complications showed no significant differences
between the two groups in spite of differences in the resources used.

It must be remarked, in concluding this chapter, that many of the
examples quoted in earlier chapters might be used interchangeably
with those presented here under the heading of 'Evaluation'. The
choice of examples in the present chapter is also arbitrary in that it
represents a tiny sample of a very large field and, within the space
available, cannot even illustrate adequately the range and variety of
the applications of epidemiology to evaluative work. The range of
possibilities is technically limitless and the limitations, such as they
are, arise generally from resistance to the notion of measuring performance or of specifying objectives in terms which demand
evaluation. The difficulties are emotional, and sometimes political or
professional, rather than technical. We shall describe some of these
problems more extensively in following chapters.

13. Misuses, mistakes, and misunderstandings

13.1. NEED FOR A BROAD UNDERSTANDING

In Chapter 11 we described the basic techniques of epidemiology and in Chapter 12 we enlarged upon its applications to health-care planning. In this third Chapter of Part III we are concerned with the limits of application, with misapplications, with a variety of possible misuses, mistakes and misunderstandings, and with their recognition and control.

The basic requirement for avoiding trouble is a fundamental understanding of the nature of the subject and an exact knowledge of its techniques. This is certainly so for the epidemiologists themselves and has important implications for designing the content and method of their training. Common sense alone is not sufficient. In health care planning contexts the epidemiologist is frequently asked to explain or interpret results in fields of application with which he has no firsthand familiarity, and to detect errors, and resolve conflicts. He must be able to do this with convincing precision and, in addition, be able to extrapolate findings from one place to another, or from the past to the future, and to understand the legitimate and illegitimate transfer of investigative techniques between different applications.

It is necessary also for the other professional people involved in health care planning to know sufficient of basic epidemiological techniques and applications to know when an epidemiologist is necessary, or at least when to ask him if *he* thinks he is necessary. The epidemiologist and administrator may have to decide jointly the extent to which a particular problem may prove tractable to an epidemiological approach or when it may be more appropriate to use different professional skills (e.g. economics, operational research, sociology, data processing, etc.), and when the overlap is sufficient to require teamwork.

This last part of Part III, in which we describe the mistakes which can be made, is in some respects an introduction to Part IV. There we shall consider and describe the alternative forms of working relationships between epidemiologists and others involved in planning, together with the arrangements through which those with epidemiological training, but without experience of health care work, can become skilled in the particular field of application.

13.2. LOGICAL AND EXTRA-LOGICAL PROCESSES

Certain of the processes outlined in earlier sections of this book have been described as 'extra-logical'; others may be described as 'logical' or 'formal'. The extra-logical processes include the construction of taxonomies, priority decision making, the formulation of models and hypotheses and their validation, the processes of extrapolating (on the basis of models) from one situation to another or from the past to the future, the causal interpretation of associations and of space–time connectivities, and the process of drawing conclusions about populations on the basis of findings within samples. The truly logical or formal procedures are mainly concerned with the coding, analysis, and presentation of information; that is, information is a material whose rules of procedure are sufficiently exact (e.g. arithmetic rules) for an observer to say objectively whether the process and outcome are 'right' or 'wrong'. These rules of procedure are highly identified with mathematics and with the logical (algorithmic) languages developed for use as computer programming devices.

Assertions that most of the scientific and practical devices used by epidemiologists are extra-logical and that logicality is largely limited to the associated mechanical functions will come as no surprise to applied scientists working in physics, chemistry, or engineering. The point must be made here, however, because widespread misunderstandings have grown up in the last few decades around the question of the putative logic of statistical inference. Indeed, some statisticians, epidemiologists, and sociologists came to believe not so much that statistical inference was out of step in being the only form of inference which had been alleged to be logical, but that statistical–arithmetical methods had revealed the logical principle whereby other forms of inference could be shown to be so.

We can only repeat the point made earlier, in § 11.6; the logic of statistical confidence calculations, and of tests of significance, is based upon an argument which moves, strictly, from a definable population with known characteristics towards the description of the characteristics of samples. There is no way of reversing this process, in logic. Thus, a statement of statistical significance must always begin with the conditional statement 'if the null hypothesis were true then. . .', and there is no way of inverting this statement to make a non-conditional statement about the parent population. Statements which omit 'if', and which declare a population value and a range of confidence, or which make statements about the probability of an estimate or conclusion being right or wrong, can *never* be justified in logic, and are made on intuitive grounds. Although it is often not recognized, the rejection of a null hypothesis on the basis of statistical arithmetic must be justified on the basis that an alternative and more acceptable hypothesis can be postulated.

Incorrect assumptions about the logical nature of the analytical process also bedevil studies of situations where multiple variables interact. Especially where computer processes are used (e.g. multiple regression techniques) there is an unfortunate tendency to believe that the selection or exclusion of primary associations on the grounds that they are 'significant' or 'not significant', necessarily has implications with respect to postulated causal links. In fact it is not so. A proper interpretation takes account of the outside world and of the corpus of tacit knowledge which already exists. Analytical processes of these kinds are more suitably regarded as techniques of display, susceptible to informal interpretation, rather than as logical pathways to inference.

13.3. TRAPS AND PITFALLS OF EPIDEMIOLOGICAL APPLICATIONS

The misunderstandings alluded to above are especially important to professional investigators with complex general problems. For example, how much weight is to be placed upon experimental demonstrations of carcinogenicity in small samples of mice in, say, ten out of a thousand tested drugs and food additives. The problem is one of interpretation, both statistical and inductive.

There are however many elementary traps and pitfalls in the design, execution, and analysis of 'simple' *ad hoc* investigation which are far less subtle; that is, a good epidemiologist should not fall into any of them, although inexperienced people frequently do so. The epidemiologist is frequently called upon to sort out the mess, or at least to detect the error and to show that the conclusion was false.

Reference was made earlier to 'cohort effects'; that is, a variation according to age of some parameter or index does not necessarily mean that this represents the natural history of the condition. Older people are, on the whole, shorter than younger adults but this means, in the main, that people born more recently have grown taller, rather than older people have shrunk. Of course there may have been shrinkage too, and, the real issue is a quantitative one: *how much* of the effect is due to shrinkage and how much is due to failure to grow. The same kind of problem applies in studying mortalities from many diseases, or the demands made by affected persons upon health services, or the results of biochemical and clinical examinations. Survival effects add further scope for error.

There is another large range of errors related to 'self-selection'. For example, women presenting for cervical cytology screening do not provide reliable indices of prevalence or incidence, because, as has been shown repeatedly, those who attend are the least likely to have the disease. Where repeated letters of invitation are sent, each new yield of attendances demonstrates a higher prevalence of carcinoma-in-situ than in the previous group. Similar selective effects can occur during the course of therapeutic trials where the 'non-co-operators' progressively drop out. If the 'controls' are not receiving a placebo treatment, then the rate and type of drop-out may be different in the two groups. In badly supervised trials, inexperienced field workers may actually transfer unco-operative 'treateds' to the 'controls'. For example a randomized trial of the effect upon breast feeding of the antenatal expression of colostrum, encountered problems of non-co-operation. The nursing staff in charge transferred non-co-operators from the treated to the control group. The non-co-operators also subsequently failed to co-operate over the matter of breast feeding itself, and the result was a resounding improvement of relative performance among those who remained within the 'treated' group, compared with the 'controls'.

Another frequent source of error relates to failure to understand the dimensionality of data. Investigations are frequently reported in which cross-sectional material, from which prevalence estimates might reasonably have been made, somehow lead to apparent statements of attack rates and even of natural history without there being any possibility of doing so. For example, many cross-sectional studies based upon cervical cytology screening programmes have made precisely the same mistake despite the fact that the error is very well known. Age distributions are presented of prevalence (at first examination) for carcinoma-in-situ, for occult invasive carcinoma, for invasive carcinoma, and for death. Arithmetic is carried out to calculate mean ages (or modal ages) for each finding and the results interpreted as a statement of the mean duration of each 'stage'. In the original data time was never measured and successive examinations in the same woman were never linked. It is easier to recognize on dimensionality grounds that it *must be* nonsense, rather than go to the trouble of demonstrating it to be so at length, although this can also be done.

Misinterpretation of before-and-after comparisons is another fertile source of erroneous conclusions. This is sometimes known as the *'post hoc ergo propter hoc'* fallacy. For example, the introduction of gamma globulin prophylaxis for Rhesus Haemolytic Disease of the Newborn was introduced widely into Great Britain in 1969. The following five years witnessed a substantial fall in the death rate and stillbirth rate from this disease. It was widely assumed that the one had caused the other. In fact, the fall had been proceeding evenly in the years before the introduction of the prophylactic procedure, and much of the subsequent fall can be attributed to changes in the birth rank distribution of the population and improvements in the care of affected infants. The true effect of the prophylactic programme, initially on a very modest scale, appeared only several years later (Knox 1976). Even where an improvement can be unequivocally associated with a service innovation, it can be very difficult to be sure that the one caused the other, rather than that the effect was mediated through some parallel pathway. The effect is usually known as the 'Hawthorne effect'. The paradigm is the observation that playing music in factories improves production, but that stopping it improves it again. Almost any attention to a service promotes increased interest and improved standards, not necessarily through the medium of the innovation itself. A recent example in a health care context has occurred in France where a major national enquiry into perinatal and post-neonatal infant mortality has 'resulted' in major improvements (Ministère (Francais) de la Santé Publique et de la Sécurité Sociale 1970; editorial comment—Institut National de la Santé et de la Recherche Médical 1973).

One particular form of selection ˋeffect, producing especially perplexing results, is when selection occurs on the basis of some hidden or unrecognized variable. For example, if the results of two educational performance tests (e.g. reading, arithmetic) are compared, they will in general show a positive correlation; children who are good at one are good at the other. Suppose now that the group is divided into three streams on the basis of the combined result, a top stream consisting of 10 per cent, a second stream consisting of 20 per cent, with the remaining 70 per cent in a lower stream. Samples taken, now, from either the upper or the lower streams will still show positive correlations between the results of the two tests. However, a sample taken from the middle stream will probably show a negative correlation; the children who got into the second stream were, by and large, bright children, who happened to perform below par in one of the two tests, on the particular day. If a sample from the middle stream were all we had, we might draw erroneous conclusions. Similar effects have been observed in many health care situations. Samples of hospital patients frequently show distorted associations between two findings. For example the patient is in hospital either because he has condition A, or because he has condition B, or both. If he has neither, he is not in hospital at all, and a 2 X 2 table to demonstrate the association between A and B will be short of cases in the cell signifying 'neither'. Another example relates to studies of the effects of smoking cigarettes. It was found in elderly men that there was a negative correlation between blood pressure and the numbers of cigarettes smoked (Brown *et al.* 1957). It was at first thought that this might be one of the rare beneficial effects of tobacco. As it later turned out, it was simply that men who smoked cigarettes *and* had hypertension were already dead. There is an analogous but slightly different explanation of the observation that Parkinson's disease is *infrequent* in cigarette smokers. Here it was the smoking itself which failed to survive.

The 'regression' phenomenon is another frequent source of erroneous conclusions. If a population is distributed according to some criterion which varies from time to time in the individual, or of which the measurement varies, (e.g. blood pressure, serum cholesterol, intelligence, blood sugar etc.), then those individuals who occupy the extremes of the distribution, with very high or very low values, do so for two reasons. That is, they normally have a rather high blood pressure and, on that particular day, any variation or error was in the upward rather than in the downward direction. If men with high blood pressure are selected and re-examined on a second occasion their mean blood pressures will tend to be lower because, although they still have a generally high level, the upward variation which contributed to their original selection, is now spread out in both an upward and a downward direction. If the patients have had some treatment in the meantime it is likely to get the credit. There may in this case be some 'settling' for psychological reasons as well, but this is a separate matter. The same applies if we take men with *low* blood pressure and remeasure them; on the second occasion the mean levels are less extreme—that is, they have 'regressed towards the mean'.

Similar phenomena are observed in associations between fathers and sons or other pairs of relatives, when we can regard the two assessments as alternative measures of a common family characteristic. If we take intelligent fathers and measure the intelligence of their sons, we find that the mean I.Q. for sons is not as high as that for the fathers, and is somewhere between the fathers' levels and the population mean. Conversely—and this is less well known—if we take intelligent sons, and measure the I.Q. of their fathers, the fathers' I.Q. will be somewhere between that of the sons and that of the general population. In other words, 'regression towards the mean' has nothing to do with time; it is a purely statistical phenomenon and occurs symmetrically in both directions, both forward and backwards.

It is neither possible nor appropriate in an account such as this to attempt a full catalogue of all the errors, or even the types of error, which beset the unwary or the inexperienced. It is intended simply to demonstrate that they exist in number and variety, and that common sense in the hands of the inexperienced has not proved, in the past, to be a reliable preventative.

13.4. SEMANTIC PROBLEMS

As pointed out in Part I, important stages in the planning process (e.g. priority decisions) are essentially political in nature, and depend upon consensus (or conflict) rather than objective and fully rational criteria. The tools of these processes are words rather than numbers. Very often the same words are used by those whose involvement stems from their profession as scientists (epidemiologists, economists, sociologist, statisticians, etc.) and those who are there to represent and to advocate a point of view determined mainly on non-scientific grounds—that is, loosely speaking, politicians. The same words do not necessarily mean the same things to both and are not necessarily used with the same purposes in mind.

Sometimes this is a matter of precision. For example the terms 'efficiency', 'effectiveness', and 'efficacy' may be used by an epidemiologist with a precision which entirely escapes a clinician (say), and a politician commenting on the 'standards' of a service may be horrified when the epidemiologist or operational research worker proceeds to dissect the concept and to write the standards down in a form which cannot be blurred. This may arise, for example, when a decision is made to introduce expensive equipment (e.g. computers, radiotherapy equipment, etc.) and where the decision has been made partly in response to the pressures of a commercial or other sectional lobby. It may have been thought sufficient to set the 'objectives' in some such terms as to 'improve the standard of patient care'. If this is to be translated into an evaluable objective it becomes necessary to specify what current standards are and what specific improvements are intended. We remarked earlier that this is not easy. In addition it is not always welcome.

The term 'experiment' is another which is widely used in a loose manner, often in an archaic sense meaning no more than to 'innovate'. Perhaps the finance comes from a research and development fund, for which word 'experiment' has to be used, but there may be no real intention to carry out investigations. 'Experiments' are quite frequently announced without any accompanying statement of what questions are to be answered, or even any realization that there should be any questions at all. 'Evaluation' is of course a word with several *legitimate* meanings and it may be based either upon the *post hoc* examination of a service which has already been supplied, or upon predicted outcomes of a model service which has not yet been supplied. Nevertheless, one thing is constant, namely that if there are no objectives there can be no evaluation; objectives *must* be defined either in advance or *post hoc* by implication. This is frequently omitted where the conceptual framework of an evaluation exercise is misunderstood, and absurdities abound. In some circumstances, for example, teams are set up to 'evaluate' 'experiments'.

Attempts have been made to clarify the issues through painstaking construction of glossaries and thesauri (Hogarth 1975), but although they have an educational value it must be regretfully conceded that the problems usually go deeper than the definition of words. Usually they are based upon a muddled conceptual framework. Some health care planning contexts involve people who are quite unused to thinking in precise terms and perhaps some who are antipathetic to health care research and who dislike the explicit discipline of posing questions in formats which can be answered. These situations are especially likely to occur in relation to subjects where the traditional approach is through conflict and confrontation. Those engaged in evaluative work quickly discover that there may be more problems in asking a question than in answering it.

The semantic examples listed above relate strictly to the English language. However, other languages provide almost equal opportunities for introducing semantic muddle, and the confused ideas behind the misuse of words are, of course, common to all of them.

13.5. MISUSES OF EPIDEMIOLOGY

Epidemiology is a sufficiently difficult subject technically, and the health care planning context is sufficiently complex, for us to be sympathetic when misuses occur. We can usually put them down to technical error, or haste, or to mutual misunderstanding between participants in the process. Sometimes, however, the misuses lead us to suspect that they have been carried out deliberately or that the perpetrators have participated in a conspiracy of muddle or of wishful thinking far below the standards expected of professionally trained people. The misuses can be classified as sins of commission and sins of omission.

Not infrequently epidemiological and statistical arguments are marshalled to promote some firmly held point of view and pressed with such force that inadvisable action is undertaken, or desirable action foregone. Some of the activities of groups opposed to the fluoridation of water supplies come into this class. The arguments contain numerous technical errors including, for example, *post hoc* selection of cities with high and low cancer rates which happen to have high and low fluoride concentrations in water supplies, and the omission of recognized procedures such as age/sex standardization. Nevertheless, in the hands of determined people, numbers can be assembled and presented with subtlety and may be sufficient to block action at administrative levels occupied chiefly by people unable to distinguish the truth on technical grounds.

Misapplications such as this do not always come from outside the health care or social administrative system. Sometimes epidemiologists working within the system can become so identified with the interests and good name of their employer as to take an over-complacent point of view. For example, regrettable laxity over enforcing asbestos dust regulations in factories has been known to occur, and a medical officer whose city was beleaguered by a refuse-collectors' strike, and a consequent plague of rats, somehow brought himself to say in public that the rats did not constitute a hazard to health.

Many errors of commission arise less from single-mindedness as from a mixture of technical incompetence and wishful thinking. Many scientific papers, for example, display good data, competent analysis, and well laid out conclusions, the only difficulty being that the conclusions are not derived from the data. Another class of investigation involves a circularity which succeeds in confirming (however covertly) the conclusions which went in at the beginning. Investigations which derive 'norms' on the basis of the existing facts come into this class. We shall have achieved an advance when we cease to be surprised that the number of special school places for educationally subnormal (ESN) children almost exactly matches the number of such children in the community.

A particular hazard of health care research is the misidentification of the benefits or objectives of a health care system. An investigator who set himself the task of maximizing the ratio of benefit to cost in a cytological screening system discovered that the best result was obtained if each person had one test and no more. This results from the pattern of diminishing returns which this kind of investment usually exhibits. The consequences of misidentifying this maximization process as a legitimate service objective, can be imagined. In another investigation concerned with the provision of hospital care for terminal illness the investigator conducted a study of the waiting list dynamics and of the proportion of dying patients who died before they could be admitted. Appropriate projections of the changing proportions which would follow upon an increased number of beds were drawn up. In fact, however, provided that a sufficiently accurate prognosis of the time of death were made, and patients refused admission until almost dead, it would have been possible to admit everyone without increasing the beds. The point now emerges that increasing the proportion admitted is not the real objective of the exercise, but rather the provision of as many days of care as possible, in patients beyond a certain stage of their disease, and in families beyond a certain stage of their endurance.

Inexpert or wishful handling of epidemiological problems interacting with economic issues is another fruitful source of misapplication and sometimes conflict. Some planners and investigators have difficulty in recognizing that there are many ways of costing a service, and they fail to distinguish between a budgetary cash cost, and a costing carried out on a different basis. They are disturbed to find that different methods of costing produce different results depending, among other things, on the question 'cost to whom'? For example, when is it proper to operate on the basis of cost to the community, or on cost to the health care service, or on cost to part of the service, such as the hospital service? The appropriate costing method depends upon the framework of the decision which it services and the purpose in mind. With respect to the latter, for example, one method of costing hospital bed-days is through simple division of the total budget of the hospital by the number of bed-days provided. This might be suitable for calculating appropriate reimbursement, whether from a central source or from privately-paying patients. On the other hand, if the decision to be serviced relates to the closure of beds then it is the 'marginal' costs which are of interest, that is, the extra costs of keeping extra beds open. Again, the answer will differ according to whether the decision is about beds, whole wards, or whole hospitals. At more general levels of decision making the problem may relate not so much to the question of reconciling budgetary accounting with different costing methods, but in redesigning the budgetary approach. Cost accountants are sometimes disturbed when planners wish to redesign the budgetary system in order to modify the form and quality of the service, rather than adjust the service to make the books balance; that is, the budgetary method becomes a tool rather than a master strategy. Clearly, there are many ways of achieving wrong results in this complex field.

One pervading misconception deserves special mention. Very often, where resources do not match demands, there is an emphasis upon 'economy' in the sense of 'saving money'. Investigations and developments are set up (e.g. information systems, closures of hospitals, altered methods of payments, disincentives to demand such as item-of-service-payments, central purchasing arrangements, centralized laboratory services, and so on) with the avowed intention of 'saving money'. Very often, too, this is a misidentified objective. Opportunities for rationalizations of this kind are frequently associated with arrangements where funds are centrally provided and where the total sum available is fixed. There can therefore be no saving of money', simply a redeployment of the way in which it is spent.

Misuses of omission, like those of commission, also range from those with essentially emotive origins to those based upon misunderstanding and lack of clear thinking. With respect to the first, the omission of, or resistance to, the research on which health care planning may rationally proceed stems from the undeniable fact that such research is always threatening, or seen to be threatening by someone. It is seen, correctly, as an agent of administrative change with the attendant suspicion—again reasonable—that some of those employed in the service may suffer diminished income, or diminished status, or will simply have more work to do. The objective is not to make administrative decision making easier, but to make the outcome better. From the point of view of the epidemiologist the forms of resistance to investigation can be very disturbing. However professional and objective he tries to be he will be treated by some people as politically motivated and the steps taken against him may be of like nature. The development of fruitful working relationships is a subject which will form a major part of Part IV.

Matters can be made worse by the fact that first entries to the investigation of a particular service are likely to criticize. It is often the suspicion that a service is defective, which provokes a situational analysis. This is what elevates the priority of an enquiry in the first place, and in any case, the first approach to improving a service must always be to find out where its defects lie. The confrontations arising from these first approaches, especially when the investigation was unsolicited by the clinical and administrative participants, may prevent further progress. The matter may remain negotiable and not all situations will prove intractable, but some almost certainly will. Much depends upon the climate in which the planning operation takes place and upon such factors as the security of the clinicians and nurses and upon local traditions. Acceptance of change based upon evidence may be quite different in adjacent specialties. Where there is widespread suspicion of and resistance to rational approaches by investigators and planners from 'outside' a particular specialty, confrontational attitudes may develop to the point where virtually the *only* goal of the epidemiologist is in demonstrating what is wrong. In other situations, where administrators, clinicians, nurses, and others prefer to see this expertise used in assisting them, the epidemiologist will have to develop a fuller range of techniques, appropriate to the whole of the planning cycle.

At less emotive levels, one of the most frequently encountered 'misuses of omission' takes the form of over-reliance upon ungrounded or inadequately grounded theory. Clinical medicine is based upon a large body of theory derived from a few basic disciplines, notably pathology, physiology, and pharmacology. Many doctors, and especially medical students, base their understanding of the natural history and progress of a disease, and their choice of treatment or advice, upon a knowledge of its pathology and upon a deduction as to what the natural history (and the most appropriate treatment) *should be* rather than on a wide experience of what it *is*. And, often, they are remarkably successful in their deductions. A great deal of the planning of services, too, must be based upon a theoretical background rather than upon a direct assessment of effectiveness. Unfortunately, the process of converting clinical procedures into well organized and effective services is a complex task, and a theoretical background which is sufficient for the clinician may not be adequate for the planner. First, medical information alone is not sufficient; the background theory must include knowledge of economic, operational, and behavioural (e.g. acceptability) components. Secondly, the medical theory itself must be supplied in a more precise and quantitative form than that which is suitable for clinical purposes. For the clinician it may be sufficient to know that the hazards of an investigation (e.g. mammography) are small. For the design of a service the qualitative issue *'whether'* may not be sufficient; it is necessary to know quantitatively *how many* carcinomas will be caused, and to relate this to the number of carcinoma deaths which will be prevented. In many instances this quantitative knowledge must specify marginal quantities; how much *extra* saving, for how much *extra* hazard, and for how much *extra* cost?

Issues of these kinds can be illustrated by considering the problems of routine tests for deafness, using 'distraction tests', in infants of about 10 months old. In qualitative terms distraction tests are known to work, are known to be carried out ideally with two people, are known to require soundproof premises, and are known to require repeating in a proportion of cases; the detection of deafness in children of this age leads to treatment which is known to be beneficial. What could be simpler than setting up a service based upon a background such as this?

In practice, however, it may be necessary to set up this service with existing premises, with makeshift soundproofing. Furthermore, not all the mothers will bring their infants spontaneously and not all will do so on request. It will therefore be necessary to seek out and test some of their infants in their own homes. Again there will be soundproofing problems, but more important still, because of the demands upon manpower entailed by these visits it may be necessary to attempt the testing with one person only (e.g. nurse) rather than two. Even so, not all children will be reached. It is difficult, in advance, to predict how many children will in fact be reached and satisfactorily tested by a combined clinic and home visit approach of this kind, and even more difficult to say how many will require retesting. It is certain, however, that not all those requiring retesting will in fact be tested and that not all of those referred to an audiology clinic, will arrive. Of those requiring repeated audiological testing, not all will return, and of those requiring and offered treatment, not all will accept or use it successfully. So how do we calculate the likely benefits of an innovation such as this? In particular, how do we calculate the marginal benefits, given that in the absence of routine testing some mothers would have noticed or suspected that their children were deaf and would have sought advice in any case? Similar problems arise in the planning of many services, and screening for hypertension supplies an almost exactly analogous problem.

Operational problems, and problems of compliance, are not the only ones to which solutions are needed. Inexact knowledge of the natural history of diseases (early diabetes, glaucoma), or of the marginal effectiveness of early treatment (mild hypertension, bacteriuria, colonic cancer), of the hazards of treatment (radiation exposure, anxiety, biopsy), and of economic aspects (BCG, CAT-scanners, joint replacement, artificial kidneys, and transplants) must all be considered in quantitative terms.

Where a service has to be undertaken on an incomplete theoretical basis—as many have to be—it is especially important to monitor progress and to check whether its performance matches up with expectation. If it does not, then we may be fairly certain that there is something wrong with the theory (e.g. the natural history may not be as believed or the acceptance pattern of the service may be excluding those most at risk), and specific enquiries are then necessary. In addition, the problems tend to change in a capricious manner as the service develops. At one stage, the problem may be in providing more laboratory facilities. At a second stage the chief constraint upon improved performance may be the accuracy of the laboratories, and the need for improved quality control. At a third stage still the main problem may be a behavioural one, a question of acceptability either for the clinicians or for the patients. Finally, the economic considerations may become overriding, raising the question whether further investment should not be diverted to another field altogether. The malarial control problem quoted earlier was of this type.

The reasons for omitting adequate epidemiological or other scientific development of inadequately grounded theories are complex. Part of the problem is simple lack of foresight, part is the inadequacy of the support, and part is due to the inadequacy of current technique. Part of it, however, reflects an inappropriate working relationship. It is still usual for staff skilled in investigation and research to be employed and located in organizations quite separate from those responsible for the health care services (e.g. in universities or medical research organizations). Professional independence, which is rightly prized, is thus maintained, so the separation has some advantages, but it is often bought at an unacceptable cost. The problems of achieving independence, and at the same time responsible involvement, constitute a crucial issue. Budgetary arrangements for research and investigation also tend to be separate from service finance. The result may be that particular health care topics (e.g. effectiveness of tonsillectomy, design of clinical records, utility of multiple biochemistry tests, efficiency of general practice maternity services, customer satisfaction with a new form of mental health service based on day care, etc.) are financed through a complex disaggregation of a general research fund, whose total amount is set on some prior 'norm'. Thus, the research resources available for a particular topic have no rational relationship with the service expenditures. Absurd situations can occur. There may be sufficient funds to undertake a large-scale service whose effectiveness has not been measured even on a pilot scale, and whose theoretical basis is in doubt, but insufficient funds either to conduct a trial of effectiveness, or to set up the investigations by which the elements of the theory might be tested. In situations where an experimental approach is needed, and where the terms of the experiment need to be changed as the service escalates, it is uncommon to encounter circumstances in which workers with the necessary skills are placed in positions of sufficient responsibility and power to achieve the necessary level of control.

These important issues of working relationships will be developed in Part IV.

Working and training relationships of epidemiologists

14. Role and environment

14.1. ACTIVITIES AND ACTORS

We said at the outset that we defined an epidemiologist as someone who practises epidemiology. This was not an evasion; in the first three parts of the book we described one of the discipline's main applications (planning), the raw materials on which it depends (information), and the techniques of the craft itself. The activity, although not the actor, was displayed in some detail.

In the present part we concentrate more upon the epidemiologist than upon his discipline. To do this we shall reconsider the planning environment and indicate those variations which have a bearing on his role. We shall also examine professional interactions between epidemiologists and those with whom they work, including politicians, administrators, and scientists. In addition, we shall examine educational relationships, institutional arrangements for the maintenance of professional standards, and a number of similar topics.

We should say at this point that we have no wish to propose a stereotype, and we recognize the wide range of mechanisms through which the epidemiological input to the planning process can be contrived. There is no requirement that an epidemiologist should always be medically qualified or that he should give the whole of his time to epidemiological work. There is nothing to prevent a nurse or other health care professional from acquiring the necessary skills. Personnel with quite different professional backgrounds may extend the scope of their work to cover parts of the field which an epidemiologist would identify as his own; they include operational research specialists, economists, sociologists, data-processing scientists, geographers, systems analysts, statisticians and others. In some organizations, also, there are medically-qualified personnel working under such titles as 'medical statistician', 'health statistician', or 'health services research scientist', whose work would not be distinguishable from that which we identify here with the medical epidemiologist.

It will have been recognized that almost all of the techniques of epidemiology, and many of its applications, can be covered by combinations of other specialists. There is nothing in our appreciation of these various professional roles to indicate the presence of a void which could only be filled by a specialist (e.g. full-time) epidemiologist.

We can say with some certainty that a planning or administrative system which makes no use of the epidemiological approach has become detached from output-related objectives and dominated by budgetary and institutional management. But we cannot make this diagnosis simply because there is no epidemiologist or medical statistician on the staff.

It is therefore necessary to seek additional grounds on which such appointments might be justified. It is insufficient to rely upon the observation that in many places epidemiologists are in fact employed in health care planning tasks. Epidemiologists are in short supply and, if an increased provision of this type of personnel is required, then it must be planned, and it will be as well if we can state with some precision what the additional grounds are.

The most cogent is the general observation that all jobs tend to be better done when they are identified as the chief responsibility of a particular person. This is not simply a question of developing the expertise necessary for avoiding errors and misunderstandings and for applying valid scientific technique. The identification of a predominant responsibility demands standards and levels of effort which cannot then be avoided on grounds of competing priorities. A part-time or non-expert epidemiologist may respond adequately to planning needs as they become defined, but may be less effective in formulating these needs, evaluating the performance of colleagues without embarrassment or rancour, and creating the 'situations' from which new planning activities spring.

The second reason for requiring specialist epidemiologists is that some of the necessary tasks are indeed specialized. They may require the use of intricate techniques, difficult adaptations of standard methods to special situations, or even the devising of new techniques. Complex modelling and simulation exercises are of this kind, also the more complicated kind of correlational study, experimental design, or cohort analysis. Longitudinal studies, particularly where it is necessary to disentangle the effects of health care services from changes in the environment, are also of this type. Specialists capable of handling these situations will not be located at every level of a health care planning system, partly because there are not enough of them, but partly because the solutions of complex problems are most sensible attempted in rather general terms; the solutions are devised in order to guide (e.g. national) policy, rather than local problems of implementation alone.

The third main reason is to advance the subject and the effectiveness of its application. This must be achieved partly through technical development and research, partly through the responsive adaptation of the planning system itself, and partly through the training and education of epidemiologists and of the users of epidemiological enquiry.

All three reasons demand a strong and independent identification of the subject and of its practitioners. This independence is necessary if we are to avoid the circular inertia which develops when trainees are trained only to do the job as it has always been done.

When we come to examine the role of medically-qualified epidemiologists we find a difficult demarcation problem. For many enquiries the choice of investigator will depend more upon his particular technical expertise or experience than upon the fact, or otherwise, of being a doctor. However, there are certain kinds of tasks for which doctors are specially suited. Those investigations and developments which require an intimate knowledge of pathological/biological processes, the workings of the professional interaction between patient and doctor, and of the attitudes and behavioural responses of doctors towards each other and towards other professionals, are specially appropriate. (This is not to deny that, for certain tasks, a non-medical viewpoint may be more suitably objective.) There are also strong pragmatic (if not strong logical) grounds for medical involvement in situations where there are questions of confidentiality, and special responsibilities related thereto. Tasks related to this range of problems are central to many planning environments and wherever this is true the position of the medical epidemiologist must also be a central one. That is, we see him as a key member of many planning teams, and as a key figure for the development of the subject and the maintenance of its cohesion, but not in a 'monopoly' role.

14.2. THE PLANNING ENVIRONMENT

In Part I we described the planning process in a synoptic and over-tidy manner. In our discussion of epidemiological techniques and applications (Part III) we retracted this over-idealized concept. There are dangers in excessively formal and synoptic presentations and the main one, here, is that the function of the epidemiologist might be identified with a demarcated sector of a rigid cyclical process. We would regard this as a serious misconception with serious consequences. The epidemiological contribution to the planning process, and the process itself, are nothing if not fluid and adaptable, driven as much by the constructive 'forward look', as by the imperatives of 'situations' imposed from outside.

As we remarked earlier, the role of the epidemiologist in relation to planning depends crucially upon the degree to which he is valued.

If, as sometimes occurs, his contribution is regarded as unnecessary or unacceptable he will necessarily take the viewpoint of an external observer. His applied technical repertoire will be limited to observational techniques and, in the main, his purposes will be limited to detecting and displaying the gross defects of the health care system. His working relationship with planners will be mainly confrontational. If, on the other hand, his contribution is welcomed, he will have opportunities for participating constructively in predictive and extrapolative studies and conducting experiments.

There is one other level at which misconceived confrontations may arise, not so much between the epidemiologist and other planners, but between the planners (including epidemiologists) and managerial staff. We have throughout this text regarded planning as a holistic cyclical process which itself incorporates the processes of implementation, management, and monitoring, but this view is not always taken. In some environments, planning is seen as an advisory function contained within management. That is, the set structure is inverted. These upside-down arrangements tend to arise where an over-optimistic view prevails of the effectiveness and of the current state of development of health care services; that is, when questions relating to methods of finance, professional and union considerations, equity, financial control, and the *manner* in which a service is provided, have attained precedence over questions of standards, effectiveness, outcomes, and the need for their vigorous development. Some of the confusions between planning and management may arise for semantic reasons, but there may also be deep misunderstandings. Whatever the meanings attached to different terms, it is essential that the objectives of a health care system should take precedence over its mechanisms.

15. Professional interactions

15.1. PROFESSIONAL IDENTITIES

We said at the outset that the scope of this book would encompass an area of professional interaction between administrators and epidemiologists involved in health care planning. It was our purpose to examine ways in which the fruitfulness of their overlapping roles might be improved in a situation where misunderstanding and competition might otherwise occur. Our discussion has also taken us into areas of interaction with other professional groups. They include managers, politicians, and personnel with a range of scientific backgrounds including statistics, sociology, economics, operational research, and electronic data-processing. Other professional groups include architects, engineers, nutritionists, accountants, and lawyers. Finally, we must not forget the members of the public, voluntary societies, school teachers and educationists, and the technicians and ancillary workers with whom the epidemiologist works in carrying out enquiries. In every case there is a working interface to be established and developed, an interface which involves joint working, mutual education, and, as necessary, the forging of relationships of consent or command.

The various professional and scientific contributors tend to identify themselves with intellectual and professional bases external to the health care system itself. They may sometimes be reluctant to remain for very long in, or at any rate commit themselves permanently to, positions which isolate them from more general scientific or academic environments. Committment to one particular field may result in them losing touch with their peers, and may even deprive them of esteem in their eyes. This is especially true where there are no established career pathways within the health care service, or where there are so few specialists that a self-sustaining 'critical mass' cannot be established. Those who do make a substantial contribution to health care planning have to identify and adapt themselves to the (sometimes conflicting) expectations and role identifications of colleagues from a wide range of backgrounds. We cannot comment on all these interactions and will do so only insofar as they concern epidemiologists. The commentary is necessarily one-sided; it may be seen in different terms by the other parties.

15.2. STATISTICIANS

Differentiation of the roles of statisticians and epidemiologists is difficult and in many circumstances undesirable. (So far as medically qualified staff are concerned the terms 'medical epidemiologst' and 'medical statistician' may be regarded as synonyms.) In many planning groups there will in any case be only one of them, that is *either* a statistician *or* an epidemiologist. Where both are available their joint presence itself implies a high level of organization, an advanced state of the planning art, and sufficient work to keep them both employed. They will tend to undertake separate tasks, and their main relationships will be with less skilled workers. The problem is usually to get them together rather than to keep them apart.

If differentiation *must* be made, the statistician displays special expertise in relation to the acquisition, analysis, and presentation of large-scale (often routine) data, in the design of new analytical methods, and in the adaptation of old ones to new tasks. He will also provide a consultancy service to clinicians and others involved in planning whose knowledge of sampling, tabulation, and similar technical topics is rudimentary. A medical epidemiologist, by contrast, will be especially concerned in the conduct of field studies requiring medical skills. He will also be involved in the interpretation of existing medical data and in relating them to biological and mixed biological/operational models. His services may also be required in situations where a medical qualification is desirable in relating to clinical doctors. Problems of medical confidentiality are sometimes satisfied more easily if the investigator is medically qualified.

It is likely also that (where both are present) the statistician will tend to serve those planning purposes which are associated with the institutional mechanisms of a health care service, while the medical epidemiologist or medical statistician will concern himself especially with services defined in functional terms. If we accept the matrix image presented in Part I of this book, we can recognize that this is far from being a precise segregation of function. In practice, a differentiation of roles will often depend upon the relative levels of expertise and the special experiences of the particular statisticians and epidemiologists who are involved.

15.3. CLINICAL DOCTORS AND NURSES

The relationships of these two classes of workers with epidemiologists are governed by two main facts. First, there are many more of them than there are epidemiologists: few will be in contact at any one time, or indeed at any time, and the terms of the contacts are mainly task-specific and of short duration. Second, it is a relationship which can be initiated from one of two directions. The clinician may come and seek advice, and sometimes partnership, in an epidemiological task which he has himself devised. (Consultancy work may be shared with a statistician, if there is one.) Alternatively, the epidemiologist may approach groups of clinicians for access to data.

The 'trading relationship' established by this two-way traffic is not always so mutually supportive as it might first appear. 'Dilution' of the epidemiologists among the much larger number of practitioners means that those clinicians who ask for and receive services are not on the whole the same people as those from whom the epidemiologist asks favours. The situation can therefore be difficult if the epidemiologist becomes identified with an administration from which many clinicians feel alienated, or where gathered information leads to conclusions with which the clinicians would not necessarily agree. Problems of these kinds are patchy, involving certain sub-areas more than others, and perhaps particular institutions or specialities. Certain clinical specialists gain the reputation (in some places) of being 'difficult'. Epidemiologists themselves may adopt defensive or aggressive attitudes, and mutual ill feelings may develop. A cautious approach is usually to be recommended, but it is not always possible to avoid 'difficult areas' and even a small minority of vociferous dissent can be extremely damaging to the conduct or outcome of an enquiry, or at the very least time-consuming and expensive. The solution is partly educational, but these problems also have implications with respect to the terms and locations of the epidemiologists' contribution, and we shall return to this issue later.

15.4. SOCIAL SCIENTISTS AND SOCIOLOGISTS

Epidemiology is itself a social science and, by implication, we refer here to social scientists of other kinds. We refer in particular to 'sociologists', although with some uncertainty, because their discipline encompasses a range of different activities and is interpreted in different ways by different people. However, we may assume a certain commonality of scientific training and experience between these sub-groups, and between them and epidemiology. There is a common basis of experience in the use of population orientated research methods such as demography and population surveys. There is also a common interest in the social, economic, and cultural determinanats of behaviour, and in the behavioural determinants of disease. In principle, therefore, there is considerable opportunity for fruitful collaboration.

Nevertheless, relationships between epidemiologists and sociologists are sometimes clouded by uneasiness. This stems from differences in their conceptions of health and sickness and in the aspects of medical care to which they attach importance; also from differences in the vantage points from which they view the provision and planning of health care services. The epidemiologist tends to adopt a medically orientated view of his problems, and this is probably true even when he is not medically qualified. The notion of 'disease' is a central concept, although it is seen in terms broader than that of a pathological process and as an interaction between constellations of biological, operational, and social processes. Measuring the incidence and prevalence of diseases in populations is a major objective of epidemiologists, also the discovery of causes and the identification of methods of prevention, care, and cure. Clinical doctors and nurses are seen as primary executive agents of many therapeutic and preventive measures, and the investigative approaches are heavily influenced by the technical capabilities and the value systems of these professional groups.

Sociologists often see things from a different point of view and instead of identifying closely with objectives expressed by practitioners take a more detached view. Interactions among clients and practitioners are seen from the position of a third party. They are interested primarily in the social construction of 'illness' (as opposed to 'disease'), the labelling process, and the mutual obligations implied by the concept of the sick role. They attach greater importance to subjective, social, and cultural implications of experience than to medical and clinical meanings. Consequently, they formulate the objectives of health care in a manner different from clinical doctors, and they are more sensitive to those effects or defects of services which are outside the range of declared medical intentions. Their assessments depend upon value systems which are regarded by doctors as peripheral. Not infrequently their evaluations are sources of irritation to practitioners and administrators when, for example, they reveal distributional inequities, or undesirable levels of 'doctor-dependency', or 'dehumanizing' aspects of institutional care. Such phenomena are usually peripheral or even antagonistic to the medical model of disease, and the results of enquiry may be as disconcerting to epidemiologists as to clinical practitioners.

Conceptual frictions such as these may produce more heat than light, but there are many areas where the skills and interest of epidemiologists and sociologists are compatible and complementary. Their approaches to certain types of problems are virtually indistinguishable. This is especially true of population research based upon household-survey methods for purposes of estimating the incidence and prevalence of disease, responses to treatment, and to attitudes, beliefs, and behavioural responses to sickness and to service provisions. Studies of disability or of factors facilitating or impeding the use of health care services, and measures of satisfaction with services, might be carried out with equal skill and equal appropriateness by practitioners in either field. The question of who does what will usually depend on who is available to do it; but for topics grounded on subjective and behavioural criteria, and neither primarily nor indirectly influenced by biological processes, there is no particular requirement for medical expertise and there is every expectation that a trained sociologist will be more suited to the task. Where biological processes are important, however, the services of the medical epidemiologist are invaluable.

Many health care evaluation tasks require both approaches and provide opportunities for joint work. Often, these opportunities relate to services provided jointly through 'health care' and 'personal social service' agencies. These services may be financed and managed through separate pathways and the liaison arrangements demand special skills. There may be discrepancies between the mutually perceived roles of planners in the two services and problems in apportioning professional and financial responsibilities. If a sociologist is providing evaluative and planning contributions to the social service agency, analogous with those provided by an epidemiologist to a health care agency, there is some danger that any administrative conflicts may engender professional cross-purposes too. High levels of professional skill and maturity are demanded of both parties to this working interface if the problems are to be relieved rather than exacerbated.

15.5. ECONOMISTS

The economist, like the epidemiologist, is a 'social scientist', and while it is possible to identify certain disparities of premise between the two, their overall conceptual backgrounds are mutually supportive. This has been true from the earliest days, and William Petty's pronouncements (1899) on appropriate ways of caring for victims of the plague, and his attempts to evaluate human life, have a very modern ring to them. Apart from the economists' common background of basic numeracy, and a knowledge of statistics, the policy issues which drew them into health care studies are also those which drew in the epidemiologists. They were the public health issues of the nineteenth century (and the later) debates about the justification for governmental intervention in health services (Fein 1971). The growing costs of health services, especially in difficult economic circumstances, have brought them both face to face with common problems, and with prioity decisions about the allocation of resources among competing uses. Models drawn from the market sector, covering such concepts as inputs, outputs, marginal investments, and marginal affects, contributed substantially to the rationale of health care planning. But economists felt less than confident when asked to help with decisions about *how* to produce health care, *what* to produce, *when* to produce it, and for *whom*. Such decisions have to be made in any economic sector, but in health care planning they have special characteristics. Because of the nature of the health 'product', and the organizational and financial structure of health care services, prices (as determined by markets) are not available as indicators of the value of the product to the consumer or to society. Bereft of a traditional support, the economist therefore seeks additional information to answer questions about the allocation of resources within the health sector. It is here, especially, that the economist depends upon the support of epidemiological enquiry.

Epidemiologists involved in planning, and forced to use economic concepts and models, are likely to feel a mutual requirement for expert consultation, support, and advice. Without it they are liable to make over-naive interpretations. For example, the apparently simple notion of calculating the 'cash cost' of a service unfolds as a very complex subject indeed. First, it may be impossible to calculate the cost for the technical reason that the accounting system does not provide specific data; thus, the effort provided by a medical biochemist in advising clinicians how to interpret reports may be inaccessible, whether in terms of cash or man hours. Second, if the costing exercise is carried out in an environment where the *total* costs of the service are fixed externally, then questions of 'cash-saving' do not arise. Planning proposals are thus detached from cash economics, and are concerned essentially with transfers of real resources. Health care economic problems are always complicated by the question 'cost to whom'. Different answers will be obtained if this is identified as the hospital budget, the total service budget, the service-plus-the-patient, or the community as a whole; and, different answers will be obtained if the investigator simply allocates a proportion of the cost of the whole service, or if he attempts to cost the proposed changes, the so-called 'marginal cost'. There is no question of one method being right and the others wrong; it is simply a question of which is most appropriate for which purpose. Superimposed upon all this is the question of discount; money spent *now* is worth more than the same money saved *later* and the discrepancy depends upon the length of time between the expenditure and the benefit, and upon the 'interest rate' appropriate in the economic circumstances. Even this may be difficult to determine and may have to be attached arbitrarily on the basis of an uncertain prediction. Finally, there is a range of questions surrounding the issue of transfer of resources, as mentioned above. Not all resources *can* be transferred; closure of a maternity hospital does not necessarily permit the opening of a geriatric unit. Transfer of funds from a large institution to a small, or vice versa, or from one region to another, or from one functionally defined service to another may have quite disproportionate effects on the two parties.

The complementary approaches of the economist and the epidemiologist, and the obligatory cross-fertilization of the two disciplines, provides one of the more promising features of the current scene. Nevertheless, in service planning, the epidemiologist and the economist do not often work together. The main reason is that health economists are an even rarer species than epidemiologists and tend to be drawn into the upper layers of a hierarchical structure. They become separated from epidemiologists, in the same way that epidemiologists tend to become separated from clinicians. Economists are chiefly involved in aggregative and distributional problems involving central government and large administrative institutions, in contrast to the normal roles of most epidemiologists. If cross-fertilization is beneficial, as we believe it is, conscious efforts to overcome these difficulties must be made and reflected in the structuring of planning mechanisms and in the definition of the corresponding professional roles.

15.6. OPERATIONAL RESEARCH SCIENTISTS

Operational research, otherwise called 'operations research' (especially in the U.S.A.), is yet another of the special social sciences. It interacts with epidemiology, and the other sciences in the group. Its scope encompasses enquiries into the ways in which a service works, into the alternative ways in which it might work, and into the consequences of alternative decisions about the different ways in which it may be made to work. There is heavy dependence upon systems analysis and the processes of formulating, validating, and using models, especially for predictive purposes. There is also a major concern with the design and use of information systems. Clearly, then, it would be difficult to distinguish the field of operational research from that of epidemiology on technical grounds alone, except in terms of emphasis.

Operational research is usually distinguished, although not too exactly, from 'work study', and from 'organization and method' (O & M) studies. The chief emphasis here is upon the use of observational methods rather than model building, and upon the investigation of the present rather than on the prediction of the future. There are differences, too, in the outlets of operational research and 'O & M studies'; the first is more readily associated with the planning process and the second more readily with managerial operations within it.

Operational research and epidemiology are distinguished more readily in terms of their broad subject matters than in terms of their techniques, and in terms of the characteristics of the models which they use. Biological components constitute an essential part of the epidemiologist's approach whereas, if they are used by operational research workers at all, they are usually regarded as secondary elements. Thus, a malarial transmission/control model, in which the biological uncertainties were of paramount importance, would usually be seen as a job for an epidemiologist; a waiting list problem or a laboratory information flow pattern model would usually be seen as falling within the province of an operational research worker. However, there are many situations in which both must take part, or in which one of them must undertake a composite task. The formulation of screening programmes, with both biological and operational problems, would fall within this class, as would certain kinds of manpower supply and training questions.

In practice, demarcation problems seldom arise. Epidemiologists tend to identify themselves with functionally defined services, and operational research workers with institutionally defined services. As with other professional interactions which we have mentioned, the problem is usually to bring the two together, rather than keep them apart.

15.7. OTHER PROFESSIONAL GROUPS

There is an additional range of special professional groups with which epidemiologists involved in planning occasionally interact. They include accountants and other financial experts, lawyers, engineers, architects, and others. As with operational research workers, and the staffs of 'management services units', they chiefly serve the *institutions* of a service rather than its functionally defined components. This, of course, is not entirely true; lawyers will be concerned with questions of iatrogenic disease, negligence, standards, and confidentiality; accountants with functional innovations; and engineers and architects with adaptations of premises and equipment serving developments with which the epidemiologist is also involved. In none of these cases, however, is the basis of the activity to be found in social science, and the models and information on which these professional work are recognizably different from those employed by the earlier-mentioned groups. Professional conversations therefore tend to be of a consultative nature across boundaries of competence which both sides clearly recognize, and there is less danger of competitive misunderstanding, or of unfortunate mutual role perceptions, than may sometimes occur between the different kinds of social scientist.

16. Differentiation of functions

16.1. DEFINITION

In Chapter 15 we studied the important professional relationships of the epidemiologist. Each of the professional groups mentioned, including the epidemiologists, maintains an independent identity with a concern for the status of its subject and the maintenance of its standards. A variety of mechanisms to achieve these ends are employed, including the establishment of scientific journals, the prosecution of research and study programmes, the awards of diplomas and other accreditations, and a range of self-appraisal procedures. Most of these activities take place outside the health care planning system. Furthermore, the greater part of each individual professional contribution to the health care planning process will be more or less independent of the others, and the interactive areas are relatively small. There is some danger that the separate contributions might fail to find an effective joint expression within a complex administrative system; there is therefore a case for the conceptual consolidation of the scientific contribution under a common rubric.

Two main non-scientific contributors to the planning process, not listed in Chapter 15, are (a) politicians and (b) managers/administrators. They were omitted partly because the extensive interaction between them and the epidemiologist is presupposed in the structure of this book, and permeates the whole of the text. Secondly, the external professional backgrounds of politicians and managers are more variable and less precisely identifiable than those of the groups we considered in Chapter 15. They are identified primarily in terms of their contributions to the health care planning process, rather than in relation to institutions outside the health care services.

So far as administrators and managers are concerned there is some confusion both of terminology and of concept. First, not everyone distinguishes between the terms, and those that do may do so in different ways. In one usage 'management' is limited to the field of personal relationships, while 'administration' is given a wider meaning, covering political, managerial, and professional functions. In another usage, 'administration' is accorded an inferior status as one of the sub-functions of management, connoting the execution of routine activities whose general form has been decided at a higher level. The identification of political contributions is no less variable.

In a highly organized large-scale service, supported from central funds, the *main* political inputs will come from government. Where there is a deliberate policy of devolved responsibility, however, additional political inputs may be provided at local levels— for example the Community Health Councils of the United Kingdom. In systems with only partial public 'ownership', political representatives may exert their influence in quite different ways, and possibly in mutually restraining ways, in different parts of the system.

For all these reasons it is impossible to conceive of any universally acceptable or any universally applicable set of job specifications for the different professional contributors to the health care planning process. The specific roles are determined in different ways in different places and at different times through a form of bargaining process (see Part I). It would be useful, however, if we could distinguish and define the general roles through which the various groups contribute, and we suggest that this can be done through defining three main functions; that is, three main inputs to the planning process. We recognize them as follows.

The first of these functions is the 'political' one. This is where value systems are generated, and where external complaints and dissatisfactions are channelled. It is from this quarter that the users of the service exert pressures for change. Legal and ethical constraints also enter the planning system here. When services are partially or totally financed from central sources, a concern with 'value for money' and with an equitable geographical distribution of resources, become important matters. The second element may be termed the 'managerial' function. We use this term in a fairly general sense to cover all the day-to-day activities of man management, building management, finance, transport management, and so on, which keep a service running efficiently. These activities are based upon the detailed interpretation of stated policy and upon the translation of guidelines and rules of procedure, into action. In one sense, the management function *follows* the decisions reached in planning, but in another it contributes to the decision process itself through providing a 'forward look' at feasibilities and practicabilities. The third component may be described as the 'development' function. Its main basis is scientific rather than operational (as it is in the management function) or value-based (as in the political input), and research activities are an essential part of it. Activities in this area are a main concern of special professional groups and, insofar as there is a concern for effectiveness, of epidemiologists in particular.

16.2. SEGREGATION

There are grounds for recommending a limited degree of physical segregation, as well as a separate conceptual identification, of the 'political', 'managerial', and 'developmental' functions. This could provide a basis for an orderly division of labour and allow the various workers to identify themselves with a clearly defined range of tasks. It might also enable a planning team to recognize specific shortfalls of performance and help to avoid duplications, conflicts, and mis-identifications of objectives.

Planning failures arising from these sources are not uncommon. For example, a failure to resolve priorities in a resource allocation exercise (essentially a political issue) is likely to divert the team into a consideration of management details, perhaps with public pro-nouncements which are contradictory to an already well-thought-out scheme. A sin of omission is thus compounded by a sin of commission. Duplicative diversions from the political into the scientific area can also be harmful. In the late 1950s in Britain, when a limited supply of polio vaccine provided the opportunity for an ethical randomized controlled trial, there was a totally inappropriate political inter-vention. The public statements of the time contrived a curious blend of terminology and of value systems in which the concepts of fair shares for all, scientific enquiry, random allocation, and calls for 'volunteers' were all mixed up. Fortunately, things were better organized in the United States and thus prevented the major loss of life which might have resulted from an indecisive evaluation.

Duplications and omissions across the managerial/developmental boundary are generally of a different character. They arise from the justifiable recognition that research generates pressures for change and that change is a nuisance and sometimes harmful. Even necessary changes will in the short run *reduce* current levels of efficiency. One of the great problems of the present time is the slowness with which research results are applied, and in some instances there is resistance to providing access to data, and facilities, on which research can be based. A major misdemeanour of research workers in the past, has been their failure to count the cost of change itself. Sometimes the costs of change, and the administrative and legal consequences, go far beyond the system under immediate consideration.

The main practical difficulties of segregation also arise at the inter-face between the managerial and the developmental functions. Politicians usually have a well-defined external 'locus' from which to make an occasional foray, and to which they may return. However, the contributors to the managerial and developmental functions often work at close quarters within a more or less homogeneous administrative structure. In these conditions the weight of the managerial function (in terms of staff, finance, premises, equipment, etc.) may swamp the developmental activity. Staff whose main expertise is in the developmental area are likely to be drawn into managerial activities and to adopt conservative attitudes of mind. This is not to accuse managers themselves of total inertia. Staff employed in managerial appointments contribute substantially to planning and to development, although chiefly with respect to institutional mechanisms. But day-to-day efficiency is their first concern. The dangers of absorbing the developmental function within the scope of management is illustrated in the United Kingdom where, since the reoganization of the National Health Service in 1974, doctors with the skills we have in mind (Community Physicians) spend much of their activities contributing to 'management teams'. This is not to say that some doctors should not find satisfying and appropriate activities and careers in management; only that this does not always cater adequately for the inputs to the planning process which we have identified as the 'development function'.

We do not suggest that the 'development function' requires total segregation. On the contrary, this would be entirely at variance with our earlier requirement that epidemiologists need to be incorporated *within* the health care planning system, and not held at arms length, as external critics. However, it is necessary to construct a niche within the administrative structure which protects them from the accountability patterns of executive line management, and allows them sufficient resources, and sufficient access to data, for carrying out enquiries. There is a need also to demonstrate as well as to encourage their scientific independence, so that it can be seen publicly that the results of enquiries have not been determined by preconceived requirements.

17. Training relationships

Epidemiologists may be taught the techniques of their craft through formal courses of instruction, but learning the applications to particular biological or service fields is a more difficult and demanding task. It requires the acquisition of a broad understanding and wide knowledge of the field of study itself and, above all, experience. In some ways, service applications are more demanding than purely biological ones. The epidemiologist specializing in a biological field (e.g. congenital malformations, mental ill health, cancer) has the advantages of an international currency of nomenclature and concept, and a commonality of approach which enables him to transfer his experience from one related topic to another. In health care planning, however, the learning task is at once more specialized and less easily transferred. The epidemiologist must not only gain a wide experience and knowledge of planning contexts in general, but a detailed working knowledge of (often idiosyncratic) local problems. This is not necessarily applicable in any other situation and, in fact, may not continue long to be useful in the present one. Neither general education nor local knowledge is alone sufficient and even both may not be enough.

Medical epidemiologists have a special training problem when compared with their clinical colleagues. No matter how well or badly clinical methods are in fact taught, they always occupy a major position in undergraduate curricula. The newly qualified doctor is usually provided with an extensive grounding in clinical method, of physiological, anatomical, pathological, and pharmacological theory, and already has a substantial experience of the problems of sick people. The same cannot always be said of teaching and experience in epidemiology and, particularly for older doctors, there may have been no teaching at all. So far as knowledge and experience of the health care system is concerned, there is again great variation. Many students probably found the subject unexciting and managed to pass their exams with a very rudimentary knowledge. In any case health care systems are re-organized from time to time, rendering previous knowledge out of date; and for doctors who have migrated from one country to another even the existing system may be totally new to them. For those with adequate administrative experience and epidemiological/statistical training, the associated disciplines of sociology and economics may still be entirely new, as may the practical arts of computing and data-handling.

A consequence of variable undergraduate training and varying ages at entry to an epidemiological career is that for most countries no single postgraduate educational system will prove adequate. Several alternative schemes may have to be offered. The training required by doctors who enter health care planning early in their careers will be different from those who contribute towards the end of a clinical career. Entrants from other disciplines may have good technical backgrounds in statistics, or economics, or data-processing, but may be deficient in relation to the biology of disease or the sociology of sickness. Nursing staff wishing to enter the field may also find themselves untrained in several aspects. For all these groups the requirements will vary according to whether they contribute to health care planning on a whole-time basis, or in a part-time (and perhaps highly specialized) capacity.

The actual content of training, and the varied usage of teaching methods, are outside the scope of this book. For epidemiologists in general (as opposed to health care epidemiologists in particular), the available methods have been laid out by Lowe and Kostrewski (1973). So far as the *organization* of training is concerned, three main approaches are available; they are sometimes labelled (1) long courses, (2) short courses, and (3) apprenticeships. The 'long course' philosophy is exemplified by the pattern followed by diplomas or masterships in public health, or M.Sc. courses in epidemiology or community medicine. Some of these courses are purely for doctors; others accommodate health professionals of various other kinds, although multi-disciplinary courses (e.g. for doctors, nurses, managers, and clinicians combined) are more often of the 'short course' type and cover limited areas such as management methods, or health economics. This arrangement follows from the constraints of accommodating the needs of the different kinds of participant; the subject matters and educational approaches appropriate to cosmopolitan groups are often fairly circumscribed. 'Apprenticeship' schemes provide the standard approach in *clinical* specialties, including general practice and nursing. They have the great advantage that the teaching/learning process is immediately to the point, although it may fall short on the requirements of generality, and tends in the long run to engender inertia rather than change. In circumstances where training schemes are totally unbacked by any formal training whatsoever, such approaches can therefore be seriously deficient. Reputable apprenticeship schemes do of course supply such backing, and its presence is a reliable mark of reputability.

No single method will meet the educational requirements of all epidemiologists. Most situations demand that all three approaches should be used and they must cater for (a) primary career education, (b) continuing (refresher) education, and (c) the re-training of those undertaking new whole-time or part-time roles. A 'multiple' approach (as followed, for example, by the Faculty of Community Medicine in the United Kingdom) could include a period of planned apprenticeship supported by modules of formal training, and followed by a period of advanced in-post training and experience, which leads to accreditation as a specialist in the subject. However, alternative pathways should be provided for those with special needs or difficulties, including one-year or two-year whole-time courses (e.g. M.Sc.), before entry into advanced training. These and similar arrangements demand the existence of a recognizable career pathway and an independently definable function in the planning system; they constitute an additional and crucial argument in favour of the partial segregation of the 'development' function.

One further dimension of epidemiological education needs special attention, namely that provided for administrators, managers, economists, and other contributing specialists. It is a difficult requirement to meet and the courses and career-training arrangements suitable for specialists will seldom provide a suitable vehicle. The most suitable format may be the 'multi-disciplinary short course' addressed primarily to topics such as managerial methods. The opportunity to introduce epidemiology (and other special sciences) is one of the cogent reasons for organizing courses of this kind.

18. Implementations

In so variable a range of situations as outlined above there can be no hope of stating and justifying any general statement of an appropriate manpower complement, either for specialist epidemiologists, or for others involved in health care planning processes. Indeed, a statement of manpower needs must be one of the objectives of the planning process itself. It is easy to see, however, that there are dangers in this.

The chief problem arises from the inertial properties of a planning system which, deprived of any absolute criterion for determining the numbers which it needs, becomes preoccupied with avoiding the embarrassments of over or under supply. That is, it is unlikely to spend effort in creating posts which cannot be filled, or to provide training and experience to fill jobs which do not exist. A tendency to match the future to the past may apply to the content of the training, and to job specifications, as well as to numbers. Changes either in training or in job specification will result in a mismatch; that is, simultaneous over *and* under supply. These phenomena are familiar characteristics of many health care systems and apply also to professional groups other than epidemiologists. Paradoxically, change may be achieved only by *creating* mismatches between supply and demand, and relying upon the effects of the pressures so created. That is, some jobs must be created or specified although the prospect of filling them is restricted; other jobs may have to be closed at the risk of some unemployment. Training programmes must be established although jobs for all the trainees do not yet exist, and the content of the training must cater for an idealized requirement, rather than the existing job content alone. The pressures must not be created irresponsibly to the point of being counter-productive, but must be related to reasonable expectations of change. All of this requires difficult judgements based upon a developed theoretical background. The provision of this background is one of the purposes of this book.

Developing first estimates of manpower needs in specific situations is a difficult and uncertain task but a necessary one, and one which has been attempted too infrequently. An example of an exercise of this type in the United States was a requirement for 2500 epidemiologists, or one for every 125 physicians; a less conservative estimate, based upon staff establishments in the United Kingdom would indicate a need for 8000 epidemiologists in the United States, or 1 for every 40 physicians.

18.2. INSTITUTIONAL ARRANGEMENTS

We suggested earlier that the contribution of the epidemiologist to planning and development will depend upon the arrangements under which he is employed and that unsatisfactory terms could stultify his efforts. There were advantages to be obtained from the separate recognition and the partial segregation of the political, the managerial, and the developmental functions, and the recognition that the epidemiological and the other scientific contributions are chiefly associated with the last of these three.

It is necessary, also, that epidemiologists should come together in groups of critical mass to provide a self-generating impetus both to the application and to the technical development of their craft. They must be able to generate and execute evaluative projects which have not specifically been asked for, and to contribute to the 'situational analysis' phase of the planning cycle in a spontaneous manner, as well as to respond constructively to the demands made upon them at other stages. There has to be a basis for the training of new recruits, for the further education of established practitioners, for the supply of consultancy services to clinicians and nurses, and for the education of non-epidemiologists in the basics of epidemiology. The arrangements must be designed to provide the discipline with a recognizable identity, with adequate status within the administration, and to provide the basis of a career structure for the technical and ancilliary staffs involved. Arrangements must be made to provide scientific workers with necessary entry to positions of (joint) control, where this is necessary, for example in the development and usage of monitoring systems, and in the conduct of experiments. At the same time they must be freed from comprehensive line management accountability as understood (often) within the management function. Their contributions to planning must be seen to be on equal terms with those of managers and politicians, rather than as subservient to them.

Several institutional devices are available. They include (i) the formal designation of a class of established posts within the service organization (e.g. epidemiologists, community physicians, medical statisticians, medical administrators, health statisticians, etc.); (ii) the establishment and recognition of one or more graduate training schemes for such staff, preferably with arrangements for in-post training experience, and appropriate accreditation arrangements; (iii) the establishment of budgets, preferably at several levels, for financing and contracting research and development (R & D) studies; (iv) the setting up of R & D units/planning units/planning-studies units. . .to provide the nuclei from which both training and research arrangements can be seeded. Ideally, all these devices should be used. We comment upon some of them in later paragraphs.

18.3. CAREER POSTS AND PATHWAYS

The main career pathways and posts available for epidemiologists involved in planning are found in the health service institutions themselves, the universities, the research councils, the charitable foundations, departments with responsibility for health care in national or in local government, and departments responsible for other social services which interact with health (education, employment, environment, etc.). These institutional arrangements are characteristically untidy and variable but this offers a number of advantages. It provides for flexibility, a wide range of expertise, and fluid informal communications between different planning contexts and different professional groups. It is necessary, however, to engineer two particular conditions if full advantage is to be taken.

The first is that the health care service itself must establish leadership in providing a recognizable career structure in which new recruits can be trained and in which more senior workers achieve both a level of personal security and a satisfying working arrangement with administrative colleagues. The second requirement is that career pathways in different institutions should be interchangeable without serious loss of benefit (e.g. pension rights) so that epidemiologists may move between university and health service posts, between health services and government departments, between government departments and research councils, and so on. Nothing but harm results when the employees of a government department are employed under quite different arrangements from those in the health services which the government department is supposed to administer, such that transfer between the two is difficult. In these circumstances transfers of staff between government and service are unlikely to occur more than once, and epidemiologists involved with the government department are more likely to be moved to other government departments than (back) into the service. It is also essential that relatively junior staff (e.g. medical epidemiologists) should be able to spend some years in a university department, or a research council unit, carrying out research and obtaining higher qualifications, before continuing an intended career in the health service; or conversely, that those with a specialized research career initially in mind, or those who decide upon this pathway at a subsequent stage, can transfer readily from a health service post to an academic one.

There are, of course, problems for individual epidemiologists in remaining 'competitive' in the eyes of a prospective employer as they move from junior to senior posts. It is doubtful whether these problems can ever be solved by the institutional arrangements themselves, but it is essential that the arrangements should not impose additional constraints. Considerable ingenuity and a substantial period of development may be required, in order to see that they do not.

18.4. RESEARCH AND DEVELOPMENT (R & D) BUDGETS

The establishment of a separate budget for R & D related to health care planning, serves to identify and to supply 'official' recognition of the need for this stream of work. To this end it should probably be specified separately from budgets for 'bio-medical' research. The division may be achieved through allocating responsibilities for the two streams of work to different bodies; the responsibility for planning R & D may lie with a government department and that for bio-medical research with a research council. Too rigid a division can be harmful; biological considerations cannot always be separated from operational aspects of planning, and research workers employed through either budgetary mechanism might have legitimate and extensive interests in the field of work covered by the other. Ingenuity may be called upon before satisfactory arrangements are developed, and quite complex cross-liaison and cross-contracting arrangements may have to be set up.

In a complex administration, with planning functions at several levels, each level should probably have its own health care R & D budget. That is, if the total amount to be spent is to be determined at a central level then only a part of the programme to be based upon it should be contracted from the centre, and the remainder distributed to 'junior' planning authorities for contracting and deployment at their discretion. It may also be desirable to allow local discretion concerning the total amount to be spent, perhaps within limits. Competent research manpower is a limited commodity and in many services it will be necessary to relate total expenditure to research capacity according to some general overall plan.

Planning authorities are sometimes able to deploy, for R & D purposes, staffs and other non-financial resources which have been acquired and maintained for other purposes. They might include staff involved in studies of 'organization and method' related to technical processes such as provision of laundry services, transport arrangements, incentive payments, and so on. At times the demands upon such staff will be considerable, they will have no spare time, and it may even be necessary to take on additional personnel. At another time, however, they may become available for R & D purposes, to everyone's mutual benefit.

In deploying a central research budget it is not suggested that each individual layer of the hierarchy should be self-sufficient, or should operate independently from the layer above it or below. Many R & D ventures are best designed around an interface between two layers. It may be possible within a large region to relate a staffing structure (e.g. for an anaesthetic service) to the quality of care, and to demonstrate in some quantitative sense what additional standards can be bought for what additional staff establishment. The staff establishment may not simply be a question of money, or of transfer from one form of expenditure to another within the region, but a matter of national policy, developed out of negotiations between a government department and a body representing anaesthetists. The regional staff establishment may indeed have been centrally imposed. Therefore, an investigation carried out regionally will have repercussions upon the validation and reformulation of a more general policy and upon longer-term plans designed to modify total available manpower. It is quite frequently observed in practice that decisions to be made at one level need to be serviced through research carried out at the level below, and that the incentive for the lower level to take part lies in the effects which the findings may have upon the formulation of general guidelines and policies.

Many research and development enterprises involve three parties— a group of research workers, and at least two levels of the administration. It is a complex situation, difficult to manage, but one which can be exploited in the following way. First, it may be envisaged as a general rule that the research team should receive budgetary support from both of the levels. This will be mainly in cash from the superior level, and (possibly) mainly in kind from the second level. Since both parties are making an investment they are the more likely to take a real interest in the results and to see that, if possible, they are applied. Secondly the research workers themselves have a degree of independence from each of the other parties, sufficient both to ensure that their findings are impartial, and that they are seen to be so. Thirdly, with respect to the generation of the work, this can come from any one of the three sources, but (beneficially) cannot readily proceed to its final formulation and execution until all three points of view have been taken into account. Where academic or research council staff are involved they can usually publish the results of their research, after consultation, without embarrassment to the other parties. The fact of independence itself creates a climate of acceptability which might not be present if the research workers were seen as 'direct employees' on an administrative group, and perhaps in danger of being seen to have bitten the hand that feeds.

Research contracting in the health care planning field has developed considerably in concept and practice during the last few years. In many fields of work the precision with which objectives are declared and agreed, and with which research methods and logistics are designed to meet objectives, has improved beyond recognition. There are still problem areas, where research is not as welcome as in others. These are typically in fields where large centrally-controlled budgets can be diverted into or out of areas of commercial interest (e.g. computers), or where the outcomes may embarrass political negotiating positions (e.g. manpower research), and in such circumstances clarity (and therefore research) is not necessarily encouraged. In less sensitive fields, however, where the principle of an R & D input to planning is widely accepted, the techniques of administering budgets for these purposes are making excellent progress.

To some extent these administrative methods have been borrowed from those used for many years in research councils and (to a lesser extent) the universities. For example R & D enterprises can be classified usually to three levels of ascending complexity, namely 'projects', 'programmes', and 'unit commissions'. The 'project' is usually understood to be a proposal of relatively short duration with quite precise research objectives and is usually based upon a resource established for other reasons, but taking up an opportunity in the health care planning field. The mutual commitments of the 'contractor' and the 'customer' towards each other are precise but limited. An example might be a university department of cancer studies, mainly concerned with the development and testing of cancer chemotherapeutic agents in animals, which then formulates a proposal for a clinical trial of a particular drug in the treatment of a cancer in man. Alternatively, a radiology department may have developed a diagnostic technique which has appeared to work in small groups of patients and now proposes to undertake a more extensive study on a more realistic servicewide basis.

'Programme' research is usually understood as a stream of linked projects united by a common theme. Where a research commissioning body agrees to support a programme the commitment is necessarily more extensive and in fact becomes rather indefinite, since neither of the parties can truly see where the programme will finish. The objectives are correspondingly more general and the more specific objectives of successive contained projects will be agreed in detail only as each new result gives rise the next set of questions. For programme support therefore, there is a need for a continuing liaison arrangement between the research contractor and the customer.

At the most general level of all, that involving 'unit' support, there may be several programmes of work and perhaps several isolated projects, all under way simultaneously. At unit level the requirement is for a 'research commission', rather than anything so exact as a 'contract', and a further level of 'liaison activities' is also required. Inevitably, the mutual commitments of contractors and customers become more intricate, more general, and longer term. The contractor finds himself demanding higher levels of security for his research staff; the customer, to some extent, loses exact control over the character of the work. Clearly, there has to be special justification for setting up units such as these.

18.5. RESEARCH AND DEVELOPMENT (R & D) UNITS

Research and development units; health services research units; planning (-studies) units—various titles are used. All are concerned to service and support the processes of policy formulation and planning, in the broadest sense. This includes a contribution to situational analysis, even the creation of the situations to be analysed, priority decisions, forecasting and projecting, choosing between alternative means of meeting objectives, monitoring, implementation, and subsequent evaluation. At the same time, it is implied in some sense that 'units' stand apart from the planning process. This is true whether the unit is established under the direct auspices of the planning authority which it serves, or in a parallel manner from some superior level, or supported from an entirely external source. It is therefore an arrangement which invokes, in the sharpest terms, the dilemma between operational involvement and scientific independence.

As we have said already, the patterns of mutual commitment between the research workers (the contractors) and those for whom they carry out their research (the customers) attain their most complex and intangible forms. The 'customer' loses the tight control which he possesses in simple situations, both with respect to levels of expenditure and in the choice and detail of investigations carried out. Especially where public money is involved, the lines of 'accountability' may appear undesirably lax. Furthermore, the research workers may, and almost certainly will, probe into areas where their efforts are not totally welcome; even when their participation has been invited the results of their enquiries may go beyond specific terms of reference and the results may sometimes be unexpected or embarrassing. For example, a research group which has been asked to enquire into the budgetary consequences of closing large mental hospitals and supporting the patients with an enhanced level of domiciliary services, may also elect to enquire into the consequences of this policy for the patients. In a research unit (although less easily within a programme or a project) they may be able to do this on the basis of marginal resources, without asking for additional funds or for access to data other than that which they required anyway.

Research units bring disadvantages as well as benefits. The most important, probably, is that available research finance becomes committed to particular broad areas of work and cannot be re-deployed very quickly. That is, a research 'customer' may find that he wishes to commission a new project but that the units to which his money is committed may not be equipped or staffed to carry it out. One of the consequent dangers, from the point of view of research groups, is that initial support may be half-hearted and the work under-invested. The security of the unit may be limited, the question of tenure and careers for research staff may remain un-resolved, and mutual resentment may build up between them and their financial sources. 'Unit'-support may also create local diffi-culties. If the research group is centrally financed by a government department (for example), it may be seen by local planning groups as serving a central rather than a local interest. The research workers may also find themselves under pressure from their central source not to 'dissipate' their capacity on problems which are seen as 'local'. Active research units tend to develop an impetus of their own which may overtake the research-generating capacity of the customers, and the customers might find themselves, for most of their time, respond-ing to the advances and suggestions made by the research group. They have little remaining time and energy for taking initiatives themselves.

It is impossible to suggest universal solutions to these problems. As with other aspects of the working arrangements of scientists in health care planning, the most helpful comment may be that their relationships are *necessarily* difficult and that this arises from the pressures which each participant brings to bear upon the other; also that there is no avoiding the necessity for these pressures. It is probably true that semi-independent research units can be effective only when there is a strong tradition of scientific application in the day-to-day workings of the service-planning function. The unit is then seen as concerned with the more specialized activities, providing support to scientists *within* the administration, and bringing the special advantages of evident independence. In addition they provide centres for postgraduate education and experience. They are the centres from which the state of the art, and the state of education of its practitioners, are largely advanced. They provide one of the basic standing resources against which programmes and projects can be formulated and developed, and tried out on a pilot basis, without a major 'first-time' commitment to staff, premises, and equipment. It is also possible to manage their internal resource deployments in a manner much more economic than when expensive staff and other resources are committed to a single end. If a programme or project is held up temporarily (as many often are), or if it aborts entirely (as some do), there is scope for immediate redeployment of staff to other work. In practice many workers in this field try to keep several projects going simultaneously for just such reasons as these, and this is much easier in a moderate-sized group of research workers, technicians, and clerical staff, than it is in a small one.

The size and constitution of an R & D unit will vary according to the circumstances. If the unit is set up on a totally 'free-standing' basis it will have to be larger than if it is set up on a 'back-to-back' arrangement with a university department, or as a partially separated service unit within a health-services authority. If its commission is relatively narrow (e.g. concerned with information systems or with economic problems), it may then be rather small and even uni-disciplinary. With a wider commission a multi-disciplinary staff will be required, perhaps half medical and half non-medical, and a rather larger group may be desirable. A cross-fertilization of different disciplines carries advantages for the research workers themselves as well as for the capability of the unit, and for the 'rarer' disciplines it solves some of the 'critical mass' problems which arise if they have to work in isolation.

The disposition of research units may require some national planning. Total expenditure within a country will be determined by manpower as well as financial limits and it will be necessary to choose between the size of the units, and their number. The choice is guided by two principles. On the one hand we have the well-tried military precept that successful operations should be reinforced at the expense of the less successful; on the other hand we must recognize the principle of equity between regions, and the observation that increasing investments in particular enterprises are often governed by a law of diminishing returns. In practice, however, the governing constraint is usually the limited availability of trained and competent staff; most units will exist habitually *below* their optimal size, they will be overworked to the point of inefficiency, *and* there will not be enough of them.

19. Conclusions

The purpose of this book, reflected in the title, was to explore the applications of epidemiology to health care planning. The limitation to health care planning, as opposed to health planning as a whole, was arbitrary and in some quarters will be seen as unsatisfactory. It was decided upon because the larger application is by now very widely accepted, whereas the health care application is still undeveloped. Indeed, it is not yet fully evaluated; it is only in the last twenty years or so that more than a very few epidemiologists began to explore this area of work and only in the last ten years that this has been reflected in health care planning arrangements on any substantial scale.

It was also our purpose to explore the professional and working interaction between epidemiologists and a range of other workers. They included politicians, administrators, managers, and a range of scientific and non-scientific professional groups. It is important to note that we have not identified 'planners' among them. We have regarded 'planning' as a global activity in which all of them are involved; all of them, including epidemiologists, must be regarded equally as 'planners'. None of them individually, nor any specially designated group, can claim prerogatives in the activity as we have described it. Thus, while we may refer legitimately to the interplay of the two activities 'planning' and 'epidemiology', we must be careful not to translate this directly into a personal division of labour. This must be arranged on a quite different basis.

On the question of the applicability of epidemiological technique to health care planning there can be no reasonable doubts. It is not reasonable to establish and maintain large-scale health care systems without applying some kind of social arithmetic, without a concern for the effectiveness and hazards of medical and nursing care, and without a passing glance at alternatives such as prevention. The techniques of making such assessments are those of social science and epidemiology is part of it. In this context, indeed, we regard it as the essential part.

The contribution of epidemiology to health care planning is essentially evaluative. As we have pointed out, the term 'evaluation' means different things in different contexts and this contribution involves all of them. That is, epidemiology is concerned with the evaluation of 'situations', with the 'prior evaluation' of alternative proposals, within the current evaluations of implementation processes, and with the *post hoc* evaluation of completed programmes. It is concerned with medical and nursing procedures, both therapeutic and diagnostic, as well as total services, and with experimental as well as with observational approaches. That is, the epidemiological contribution to health care planning is by no means limited to a particular sector of a schematic planning cycle and is appropriate to all phases of the activity.

Who provides the epidemiological input? This is a question quite separate from those relating to the nature of the input and the need for it. It cannot be answered in any universal way and the solution will depend upon the situation. We envisage situations in which a statistician, an economist, a clinician, or a management-services group may be capable of meeting the need. We would not wish to assert that a specialist epidemiologist is *always* necessary, at every planning level, and it would be unrealistic at the present time to suppose that a sufficient number of epidemiologists experienced in this field could be provided. Nevertheless, there are strong grounds for building up a cadre of specialists. Appropriate job specifications will differ in different countries but they will need to be expert in many aspects of planning and administration, and in the maintenance of information systems, as well as epidemiology. They will require special training schemes in order to meet these specifications and they cannot simply be moved from one field of application to another. So far as the service and its planning mechanism are concerned, appropriate career posts and pathways, and appropriate training and re-training arrangements, will have to be devised.

There is also a strong case for setting up a limited number of research units for providing planning support, manned both by epidemiologists and by other scientists. They are capable of providing major support to training schemes, and serve to develop the theoretical and conceptual background of health care research. They provide a research resource which can tackle *ad hoc* problems at relatively short notice, as well as conducting planning and policy studies. These units require ingenious and flexible arrangements providing a degree of independence combined with integral involvement of staff members in a range of planning activities.

Finally, there is a need for a range of professional associations, to provide initiatives in this field. They must help develop both job specifications and training needs and, where appropriate, to codify and administer specialized accreditation procedures. Excessive formality can of course be harmful, especially where job specifications are designed more to accommodate existing staff than to meet future needs. Nevertheless some kind of career pathway will have to be designed if staffing needs are to be met. An institutional focus will have to be defined if appropriate staff complements are to be developed and if the planning roles of epidemiologists and other specialists are to be adapted effectively towards the needs of health care services.

References

Abel-Smith, B. (1967). *An international study of health expenditure.* WHO Public Health Papers, No. 32. Geneva.

Acheson, E.D. (1967). *Medical record linkage.* Published for the Nuffield Provincial Hospitals Trust by the Oxford University Press.

Acheson, R.M., Crago, A., and Weinerman, E.R. (1971). Institutional and social care of the arthritic. *J. Chron. Dis.,* 23, 843-60.

—— and Fairbairn, A.S. (1971). Record linkage in studies of cerebrovascular disease in Oxford, England. *Stroke,* 2, 48-57.

Alderson, M.R. (1975). The application of health information systems to planning. *Proceedings of MEDIS, 1975, international symposium on medical information systems,* Tokyo, 7-9 October 1975, pp.165-75.

Ashley, J.S.A. (1972). Present state of statistics from hospital in-patient data and their uses. *Brit.J.prev. soc. Med.,* 26, 135-47.

Atsumi, K. (ed.) (1973). *Medical thermography.* University of Tokyo Press, Tokyo.

Bailey, N.T.J. (1975). Systems modelling in health planning. In *Systems aspects of health planning* (ed. N.T.J. Bailey and M. Thompson). The proceedings of a conference held at the International Institute of Applied Systems Analysis, North-Holland, Amsterdam.

—— and Thompson, M. (eds.) (1975). *Systems aspects of health planning.* The proceedings of a conference held at the International Institute of Applied Systems Analysis, North Holland, Amsterdam Publishing Co.

Banagee, D. (1974). *Health behaviour in rural populations.* J.N.U., New Delhi.

Bernhardt, E. (1971). *Trends and variations in Swedish fertility: A cohort study,* Vol. (SCB) No. 5. U.R. Stockholm.

Bradshaw, B.R., Vonderhaar, W.P., Keeney, V.T., Tyler, L.S., and Harris, S. (1976). Community-based residential care for the minimally impaired elderly: a survey analysis, *J. Am. Geriat. Soc.,* 24 (9), 423-9.

Breslow, L. (1965). Studies in a total community. Alameda and Contra Costa Counties, California. In *Comparability in international epidemiology* (ed. R.M. Acheson), New York. *Milbank mem. Fd Quart.,* 43, 317-25.

Brett, G.Z. (1968). The value of lung cancer detection by six-monthly chest radiographs, *Thorax,* 23, 414-20.

Brooke, E.M. (1974). *The current and future use of registers in health information systems.* WHO Offset Pub. No. 8, Geneva.

Brown, R.G., McKeown, T., and Whitfield, A.G.W. (1957). Environmental influences affecting arterial pressure in males in the seventh decade, *Can. J. Biochem. Physiol.,* 35, 897-911.

Bywaters, J.L. and Knox, E.G. (1976). The organization of breast cancer services, *Lancet,* 1, 849-52.

Campbell, D.T. and Stanley, J.C. (1963). *Experimental and quasi-experimental designs for research.* Rand McNally College Publishing Co., Chicago.

Chadwick, J. and Mann, W.N. (1950). *The medical works of Hippocrates. A new translation from the original Greek made especially for English readers.* Blackwell Scientific Publications, Oxford.

Chapman, B.L. (1970). Hospital mortality of myocardial infarction, before and after coronary care. *Med. J. Aust.*, **1**, 833-7.

Clements, F.W., Gibson, H.B., and Howeler-Coy, J.F. (1968). Goitre studies in Tasmania: 16 year's prophylaxis with iodine. *Bull. Wld. Hlth. Org.*, **38**, 297-318.

Cochrane, A.L. (1972). *Effectiveness and efficiency: random reflections on health services.* The Rock Carling Fellowship, Nuffield Provincial Hospitals Trust, London.

Colombia, Ministry of Public Health (1972). *Estudio de instituciones de atencion medica — Directorio Nacional*, Serie II, No. 5. Instituto Nacional para Programas Especiales de Salud; Associacion Columbiana de Facultades de Medicina, Bogota.

—— and Colombian Association of Medical Schools (1967). *Study on health manpower and medical education in Colombia, I. methodology.* Document prepared for the International Conference on Health Manpower and Medical Education, Maracay, Venezuela, 19-23 June, 1967, Washington, D.C., Regional Office of the WHO, Pan American Health Organization, Pan American Sanitary Bureau, pp.64-8.

Cosin, L.Z. (1956). The organization of a day hospital for psychiatric patients in a geriatric unit, *Proc. R. Soc. Med.*, **49**, 237-44.

Cummings, N.H. and Follette, W.T. (1968). Psychiatric services and medical utilization in a prepaid health plan setting: II. *Med. Care*, **6**, 31-41.

Cutler, J.L., Rauncharan, S., Feldman, R., Siegelaub, A.B., Campbell, B., Friedman, G.D., Dales, L.G., and Collen, M.F. (1973). Multiphasic check-up evaluation study, 1-4, *Prev. Med.*, **2**, 197.

Dawber, T.R., Moore, F.E., and Mann, G.V. (1957). Coronary heart disease in the Framingham study, *Am. J. publ. Hlth*, **47**, Suppl. 4., 4-24.

Declaration of Geneva (1949). *World. Med. Assoc. Bull.*, **1**, 15.

Declaration of Helsinki (1964). World Medical Association, Committee on Medical Ethics, *World. Med. J.*, **11**, 28.

DHEW (Department of Health, Education, and Welfare) (1972). *Uniform hospital abstract: minimum basic data set.* U.S. National Committee on Vital and Health Statistics, Government Printing Office, Washington, D.C.

—— (1975). *The national ambulatory medical care survey: 1973 summary.* National Centre for Health Statistics, Government Printing Office, Washington, D.C.

—— (1975). *Report of the technical consultant panel on environmental health statistics.* U.S. National Committee on Vital and Health Statistics.

—— (1976). *Baselines for setting health goals and standards.* Public Health Service Health Resources Administration, publication no. (HRA) 76-640.

DHSS (Department of Health and Social Security (1976). *Prevention and Health, everybody's business: a reassessment of public and personal health.* H.M.S.O. London.

Donabedian, A. (1966). Evaluating the quality of medical care, *Milbank mem. Fd Quart., Part 2 (Suppl.)*, **44**, 166-206.

—— (1973). *Aspects of medical care administration specifying requirements for health care.* Published for the Commonwealth Fund by Harvard University Press, Cambridge, Massachusetts.

Dy, F.J. (1954). Present status of malaria control in Asia, *Bull. Wld. Hlth. Org.*, **11**, 725-63.

Edelstein, L. (1943). The Hippocratic Oath, *Bull. Hist. Med. Suppl. 1.*

Elder, R., and Acheson, R.M. (1970). Newhaven survey of joint diseases. XIV. Social class and behaviour in response to symptoms of osteoarthritis. *Milbank mem. Fd. Quart.*, **48**, 440-502.

Etheridge, M.J. (1971). Rehabilitation and heart disease, *Notes on cardiovasculor Disease*. National Foundation of Australia.

Exton-Smith, A.N. (1962). Progressive patient care in geriatrics, *Lancet*, 1, 260–2.

Fein, R. (1971). On measuring economic benefits of health care programmes in *Medical history and medical care*. Published for the Nuffield Provincial Hospitals Trust by Oxford University Press, London.

Follette, W.T., and Cummings, N.A. (1967). Psychiatric services and medical utilization in a prepaid health plan setting. *Med. Care*, 5, 25–35.

Frost, W.H. (1927). *Public health-preventive medicine*, Vol. 2., Chapter 7. Nelson-Lowe-Leaf System, New York.

Fry, J. (1966). *Profiles of disease. A study in the natural history of common diseases*. E. and S. Livingstone Ltd., Edinburgh.

—— and Farndale, W.A.J. (1972). *International medical care*. Medical and Technical Publishing Co. Ltd., Oxford and Lancaster.

Fuchs, V.R. (ed.) (1972). *Essays in the economics of health and medical care, Columbia, Natl. Bur. Econ. Res., human resources and social institutions Ser. No. 1*. Columbia University Press, New York.

Glass, N. (1976). The meaning of the term need. In *Health information, planning and monitoring*. (ed. R.M. Acheson, D.J. Hall, and L. Aird). Oxford University Press.

Goldschmidt, P.G. (1976). A cost-effectiveness model for evaluating health care programs: application to drug abuse treatment, *Inquiry*, 13, No. 1.

Gordis, L. (1973). Effectiveness of comprehensive-care programs in preventing rheumatic fever, *New Engl. J. Med.*, 289, 331–5.

Government of India (1974). *Studies on population and family planning in India*, Ministry of Family Planning and Health.

Gwynne, H. (1975). *Towards the development of indicators of needs for use in health service planning*. Division of Health Services Research, Health Commission of New South Wales, Australia.

Hall, T.L. and Mejia, A. (eds.) (1978). *Health manpower planning: principles, methods, issues* WHO Publication, Geneva. 127–51, 79–99.

Hay, A. (1976a). Toxic cloud over Seveso. *Nature*, 262.

—— (1976b). Seveso: the aftermath. *Nature*, 263.

—— (1976c). Seveso: the problems deepen. *Nature*, 264.

Henderson, D.A. (1976). The eradication of smallpox, *Sci. Am.*, 235, 25–33.

Hetzel, B.S. (1971). The epidemiology of suicidal behaviour in Australia. *Aust. N.Z. J. Psychiat.*, 5, 156–66.

Hicks, D. (1976). *Primary health care*. (H.M.S.O., London).

Hobbs, M.S.T., Fairbairn, A.S., Acheson, E.D., and Baldwin, J.A. (1976). Study of disease associations from linked records, *Brit. J. prev. soc. Med.* 30, 141–50.

Hogarth, J. (1975). *Glossary of health care terminology*. WHO Regional Office for Europe, Copenhagen.

Hyman, H.H. (1976). *Health planning: a systematic approach*. Aspen Systems, U.S.A.

IFIPTC (International Federation for Information Processing Technical Committee Four) (1975). *Considerations on the subject 'data protection'*, Report on the Fourteenth Meeting on Information Processing in Medicine, 1–2 April 1975, Budapest.

Indian Council of Medical Research (1959). *Tuberculosis in India, a sample survey, (1955–58)*. New Delhi.

Institut National de la santé et de la recherche médicale (1973). (Editorial comment),

Statistique des causes médicales de décès. Tome 1: resultats. France.

Kamat, S.R., Dawson, J.J.Y., Devadatta, S., Fox, W., Janardhanam, B., Radha-krishna, S., Ramakrishnan, C.V., Somasundaram, P.R., Stott, H., and Velu, S. (1966). A controlled study of the influence of segregation of tuberculosis patients for one year on the attack rate of tuberculosis in a 5-year period in close family contacts in South India, *Bull. Wld. Hlth. Org.*, 34, 517-532.

Kelsey, J. L. (1975). An epidemiological study of the relationship between occupations and acute herniated lumbar intervertebral discs, *Int. J. Epidem.* 4, 197.

Kessler, I.I. and Levin, M.I. (1970). *The community as an epidemiological laboratory.* The Johns Hopkins Press, Baltimore.

Kessner, D.M. and Kark, C.E. (1973). *A strategy for evaluating health services.* Institute of Medicine, National Academy of Sciences, Washington, D.C.

Kisten, H. and Morris, R. (1972). Alternatives to institutional care for the elderly and disabled. *Gerontologist*, 12, 139.

Knox, E.G. (1973). Computer simulations of cervical cytology screening programmes, In *The future and present indicatives* (ed. G. McLachlan). Published for the Nuffield Provincial Hospitals Trust by the Oxford University Press, London.

——— (1974). Multiphasic screening. *A Series from the Lancet, Oct. 5-Dec. 21, 1974*, pp. 39-42.

——— (1975). Security standards for computer medical records. In *Probes for health* (ed. G. McLachlan), pp.157-77. Published for the Nuffield Provincial Hospitals Trust by the Oxford University Press, London.

——— (1976). Control of haemolytic disease of the newborn, *Brit. J. prev. soc. Med*, 30, 163-9.

——— and Mahon, D.F. (1970). Evaluation of *infant at risk* registers. *Arch. Dis. Childh.*, 45, 634-9.

——— Morris, J.N., and Holland, W.W. (1972). Planning medical information systems in a unified health system. *Lancet*, 2, 696-700.

Kushlick, A. and McLachlan, G. (eds.) (1974). *Positions, movements and directions in health services research.* Published for the Nuffield Provincial Hospitals Trust by the Oxford University Press, London.

——— (eds.) (1976). *Approaches to action: a symposium on services for the mentally ill and handicapped.* pp.81-104. Published for the Nuffield Provincial Hospitals Trust by the Oxford University Press, London.

Lalonde, M. (1974). *A new perspective on the health of Canadians: a working document.* Government of Canada, Catalog. No. H31-1374, Ottawa.

Lavere, G.J. (1976). The ethical aspects of medical privacy. *J. Clin. comput.*, 6, (1) 23-46.

Lawrence, P.R. and Lorsch, J.W. (1967). *Organization and environment.* Harvard University Press, Cambridge, Massachusetts.

Lefroy, R.B. (1967). *The frail aged.* Consultation Report for Australian Frontier Inc., A.C.T., Canberra.

——— and Page, J. (1972). Assessing the needs of elderly people: experiences of a geriatric service, *Med. J. Aust.*, 2, 1071-5.

Lenz, W. (1961). *Tagung der Rheinisch-Westfälischen Kinderärztevereinigung in Düsseldorf.*

——— and Knapp, K. (1962). Foetal malformations due to Thalidomide, *Ger. Med. Mthly.*, 7, 253-8.

Lowe, C.R. and Kostrzewski, J. (1973). *Epidemiology: A guide to teaching methods.* International Epidemiological Association in collaboration with World Health Organization, Churchill Livingstone, Great Britain.

McBride, W.G. (1961). Thalidomide and congenital abnormalities. *Lancet*, ii, 1358.

McDonald, A.D., Gorbett McDonald, J., Salter, M.A., and Enterline, P.E. (1974). Effects of Quebec Medicare on physician consultation for selected symptoms. *New Engl. J. Med*, 291, 649–52.

McKeown, T. and Cross, K.W. (1969). Responsibilities of hospitals and local authorities for elderly patients, *Brit. J. prev. soc. Med.*, 23, 34–9.

—— (1976). *The role of medicine: dream, mirage or nemesis?* The Rock Carling Fellowship, Nuffield Provincial Hospitals Trust, London.

McMichael, A.J. and Hetzel, B.S. (1974a). An epidemiological study of the mental health of Australian university students, *Int. J. Epidem.*, 3, 125–234.

—— —— (1974b). Patterns of help-seeking for mental illness among Australian university students: an epidemiological study. *Soc. Sci. Med.*, 8, 197–206.

Martin, D.A. (1964). The disposition of patients from a consultant general medical clinic, *J. chron. Dis.*, 17, 837–45.

Mather, H.G., Pearson, M.G., Read, K.L.Q., Shaw, D.B., Steed, G.R., Thorne, M.G., Jones, S., Querrier, C.J., Eraut, C.G., McHugh, P.M., Chowdhury, M.K., Jafray, M., and Wallace, T.J. (1971). Acute myocardial infarction: home and hospital treatment. *Brit. med. J.*, 3, 334–8.

—— Morgan, D.C., Pearson, N.G., Read, K.L.Q., Shaw, D.B., Steed, G.R., Thorne, M.G., Lawrence, C.J., and Riley, I.S. (1976). Myocardial infarction: a comparison between home and hospital care for patients. *Brit med. J.*, 1, 925–9.

Matthew, G.K. (1971). Measuring need and evaluating services. In *Portfolio for health: problems and progress in medical care*, Ser. 6 (ed. G. McLachlan). Published for the Nuffield Provincial Hospitals Trust by the Oxford University Press, London.

Mejia, A., Pizurki, H., and Royston, E. (1978). *Physician and nurse migration: analysis of policy implications.* Report of a World Health Organization Study, WHO (in press).

Meyer, M.B., Tonascia, J.A., and Buck, C. (1975) The interrelationship of maternal smoking and increased perinatal mortality with other risk factors. *Am. J. Epidem.*, 100, 443–52.

Ministère (Français) (1970). *La perinatalité* (étude de R.C.B.). Pour une politique de la sante Ministere de la Santé Publique et de la Securite Sociale.

Munan, L., Vobecky, J., and Kelly, A. (1974). Population health care practices: an epidemiologic study of the immediate effects of a universal health insurance plan. *Int. J. Hlth. Servs.* 4, (2).

Murnaghan, J.H. (1974). Health services information systems in the United States today. *New Engl. J. Med.*, 290, 603–10.

—— (1976). Review of the conference proceedings on long-term health care data. *Med. Care*, Suppl. 5, 14, 1–25.

—— and White, K.L. (eds.) (1970). Hospital discharge data, report of the Conference on Hospital Discharge Abstracts Systems. *Med. Care, Suppl. 4.* 8.

—— —— (1971). Hospital patient statistics: problems and prspects. *New Engl. J. Med.*, 284, 822–28.

Murphy, E.A., and Abbey, H. (1967). The normal range — a common misuse, *J. chron. Dis.*, 20, 79–88.

Myer, M.B., Jonas, B.S., and Tonascia, J.A. (1976). Perinatal events associated with maternal smoking during pregnancy, *Am. J. Epidem.*, 103, 464–76.

Nozick, R. (1974). Anarchy, state, and utopia. *Basic Books Inc., New York.*

Oliver, R.G. and Hetzel, B.S. (1972). Rise and fall of suicide rates in Australia: relation to sedative availability. *Med. J. Aust.* 2, 919–23.

———— ———— (1973). An analysis of recent trends in suicide rates in Australia. *Int. J. Epidem.*, 2, 91–101.

OPCS (Office of Population Censuses and Surveys) (1973). *Morbidity statistics from general practice*, Second national study, Preliminary report on methods. HMSO, United Kingdom.

Opit, L.J. and Crawford, J.S. (1975). Obstetric anaesthesia: a regional audit. *In Probes for health*, (ed. G. McLachlan), pp. 47–68. Published for the Nuffield Provincial Hospitals Trust, London.

Petty, W. (1899). *The economic writings of Sir William Petty*. Cambridge University Press.

Pickles, W.N. (1939). *Epidemiology in country practice*. Simplin Marshall Ltd., London.

Pole, D.J. (1972). Myocardial infarction: methods, validity, and preliminary experience of a coronary register. *Med. J. Aust.*, 2, 1481–4.

Rawls, J. (1973). *A theory of justice*. Oxford University Press, London.

Reynolds, I., Di Gusto, J., and McCulloch, R. (1976). *A review of New South Wales Health Commission treatment services for narcotic dependent persons*. Division of Health Services Research, No. 77/1.

Robinson, J.S., and McLean, A.C.J. (1970). Mobile coronary care. *Med. J. Aust.*, 2, 439.

Royal Society of Medicine and Royal Society of Medicine Incorporated (1973). *Anglo-American conference on drug abuse*. Proceedings of a Conference held in London, 16–18 April, 1973.

Samuels, G.J. (1972). *Infringements of the individual's privacy*, pp.32–9. Proceedings of the Sixth International Congress on Medical Records, Sydney.

Schaefer, M. (1974). *Administration of environmental health programmes: a system review*. WHO Public Health Papers, No. 59. Geneva.

Schneider, W. (1976). The application of computer techniques in health care. *Computer programmes in biomedicine*, Vol. 5, No. 3. North-Holland, Amsterdam.

Shapiro, S., Strax, P., Venet, L., and Venet, W. (1973). Changes in 5-year breast cancer mortality in a breast cancer screening program. *Proceedings of the Seventh National Cancer Conference, Philadelphia*, pp.663–78. J.B. Lippincott, Toronto.

Shaw, S. (1975). The role of the nurse in assessing the health of elderly people. In *Probes for health* (ed. G. McLachlan). Published for the Nuffield Provincial Hospitals Trust by Oxford University Press, London.

Smits, H., Draper, P., and Chir, B. (1974). Care of the aged: an English lesson? *Ann. intern. Med.*, 80, 747.

South-east London screening group (1977). A controlled trial of multiphasic screening in middle-age: results of the south-east London screening study. *Int. J. Epidem.*, 6, 357–63.

Speizer, F.E., Doll, R., and Heaf, P. (1968a). Observations on recent increase in mortality from asthma. *Brit. med. J.*, 1, 335–9.

———— ———— ———— and Strang, L.B. (1968b). Investigation into use of drugs preceding death from asthma. *Brit. med. J.*, 1, 339–43.

Spitzer, W.O., Sackett, D.L., Sibley, J.C., Roberts, R.S., Kergin, D.J., Hackett, B.C., and Olynich, A. (1974). The Burlington randomized trial of the nurse practitioner. *New Engl. J. Med.*, 290, 251–6.

Springer, E.W. (1971). *Automated medical record and the law*. Aspen Systems Corporation, Pittsburgh.

Stanbury, J.B., Ermans, A.M., and Hetzel, B.S. (1974). Endemic goitre and cretinism: public health significance and prevention, *WHO Chron.*, 28, 220-8.

Tooth, G.C. and Brooke, E.M. (1961). Trends in the mental hospital population and their effects on future planning. *Lancet*, 1, 710-3.

Trikojus, V.M. (1974). Some observations of endemic goitre in Tasmania and Southern Queensland. *NZ med. J.*, 80, 491-2.

United Nations (1965). *Handbook on population census methods.* Vols. 1-3. U.N. Statistical Office, New York.

—— (1967). *Principles and recommendations for the 1970 population censuses.* Statistical Papers Series M.44. U.N. Statistical Office, New York.

Vulcan, P. (1973). *Australia's safety belt use of laws: the results of the law.* Proceedings of the National Safety Belt Usage Conference, Washington, D.C.

Watts, S.P. and Acheson, E.D. (1967). Computer method for deriving hospital in-patient morbidity statistics based on the person as the unit. *Brit. med. J.*, 4, 476-7.

White, K.L. (1973). Priorities for health service information, *Hlth. Servs. Rep.*, 888, (2).

—— (1976). In *Epidemiology as a fundamental science: its uses in health services planning, administration, and evaluation* (eds. K.L. White and M.M. Henderson). Oxford University Press, New York.

—— Anderson, D.O., Kalimo, E., Kleczkowski, B.M., Purola, T., and Vukmanovic, C. (1977). *Health services: concepts and information for national planning and management.* WHO Public Health Papers No. 67, Geneva.

—— and Murnaghan, J.H. (1970). Health services planning: models and means. *Hlth. Servs Res.*, 5, 304-7.

Whitmore, R., Durward, L., and Kushlick, A. (1975). Measuring the quality of residential care. *Behav. Res. Ther.*, 13 (4), 227-36.

Wildavsky, A. (1975). *Budgeting: a comparative theory of budgetary process.* Little, Brown and Co., Waltham, Massachussetts.

Wilensky, H.L. (1967). *Organizational intelligence: knowledge and policy in government and industry.* Basic Books, New York and London.

Williamson, J., Stokoe, I.H., Gray, S., Fisher, M., Smith, A., McGhee, A., and Stephenson, E. (1964). Old people at home: their unreported needs. *Lancet*, 1, 1117-20.

Wing, J.K. and Hailey, A.M. (eds.) (1972). *Evaluating a community psychiatric service.* Oxford University Press, London.

World Health Organization, Regional Office for Europe (1971). *Information on health and medical services.* pp.24-9. Report of the Third European Conference on Health Statistics, Turin, EURO 4910, Copenhagen.

—— (1972). Health planning and organization of medical care. *Public Health in Europe*, 1, 39.

World Health Organization, Regional Office for South-East Asia (1966). *A short study of primary health centres: in-patient, bed strength, staffing, and allied matters.* Unpublished document SEA/PHA/56.

World Health Organization (1960). *Expert committee on tuberculosis.* Technical Report Series, No. 195, 195(4). Geneva.

—— (1964). *Export committee on tuberculosis.* Technical Report Series, No. 290. Geneva.

—— (1969). *Thirteenth report of the expert committee on health statistics.* Technical Report Series, No. 429. Geneva.

—— (1971). *Fourteenth report of the expert committee on health statistics.* Technical Report Series, No. 429. Geneva.

———— (1976). *Application of systems analysis to health management.* Technical Report Series, No. 596. Geneva.

———— (1972). *Health hazards of the human environment.* Geneva.

———— (1978a). Smallpox surveillance. *Wkly. epidem. Rec.* 53, 9–20.

———— (1978b). Eradication of smallpox in India, *SEA/Smallpox/78,* Report of the International Smallpox Assessment Commission, 6–20 April 1977.

———— (1978c). Multinational study on the International Migration of Physicians and nurses.....

WONCA (World Organization of National Colleges, Academies, and Academic Associations of General Practitioner/Family Physicians) (1975). *International classification of health problems in primary care.* American Hospital Association, Chicago.

Index